NORWEGIAN-AMERICAN STUDIES

The Journal of the Norwegian-American Historical Association

2020

Since 1926, the Norwegian-American Historical Association's journal *Norwegian-American Studies* has detailed and interpreted the Norwegian-American experience. It remains focused on showcasing new scholarship in the field of Norwegian-American studies, including the related fields of history, literature, religion, art, and cultural studies. The journal aims to not only publish scholarship on Norwegian-American life, but also facilitate intellectual exchange by publishing original research articles alongside discussions of scholarly works in progress, the teaching and learning of Norwegian-American studies, reviews of books recently published in the field, and more.

Norwegian-American Studies (ISSN 0078-1983) is published annually in the fall (Northern hemisphere) by the University of Minnesota Press and is a benefit of membership in the Norwegian-American Historical Association. For current subscription rates please see our website: http://www.upress.umn.edu. Digital subscriptions are available online through the JSTOR Current Scholarship Program at http://www.jstor.org/r/umnpress.

If ordering by mail, please make checks payable to the University of Minnesota Press and send to

Norwegian-American Studies
University of Minnesota Press
111 Third Avenue South, Suite 290
Minneapolis, MN 55401-2520

Address subscription orders, changes of address, and business correspondence (including requests for permission and advertising orders) to the University of Minnesota Press, attention *Norwegian-American Studies*.

Author guidelines and submission preparation materials can be found on the Norwegian-American Historical Association website at https://naha.stolaf.edu/pubs/guidelines.htm. Direct submissions to the journal editor at naha-editor@stolaf.edu.

The Norwegian-American Historical Association (NAHA) is internationally recognized for its major role in furthering the academic study of Norwegian Americans. Since its founding in 1925, NAHA has been dedicated to collecting, preserving, and interpreting the Norwegian-American experience. The NAHA Archives are the largest designated repository for materials about Norwegian-American history and culture in North America. The Association also boasts a robust publications program, including the publication of notable book manuscripts, the academic journal, *Norwegian-American Studies*, and a quarterly newsletter. NAHA's work is supported by an active and thriving membership. NAHA is located in the Rolvaag Library on the St. Olaf College campus in Northfield, MN. To learn more, please visit its website, naha.stolaf.edu.

Cover art: Caroline Marie Stuverud Short stands at the grave of her son Lloyd Short in an American cemetery near Paris, ca. 1930. Lloyd was an American serviceman killed in action in July 1918. From the Sidney G. Sønneland Papers, 1877–1981 (P753). Courtesy of the Norwegian-American Historical Association, Northfield, Minnesota.

NORWEGIAN-AMERICAN
HISTORICAL ASSOCIATION

CONTENTS

Norwegian-American Studies 38 • 2020

EDITOR'S NOTE

This special issue of *Norwegian-American Studies* focuses on war in the twentieth century. As the image on the front cover attests, war has many consequences, many of them devastating on both individual and collective levels. While operational tactics and battles are central to the history of war, this issue delves deeper into the social facets of war. It explores the varied effects war had on Norwegian-American individuals and communities, and details the ways in which they responded to the shifting circumstances in which they found themselves.

World War Two anchors this volume. As war broke out in Europe in 1939, Norwegian Americans eagerly consumed news of the German invasion of Poland and the Russian war with Finland, termed the Winter War. Terje Joranger and Daron Olson compare urban and rural Norwegian-American newspapers' treatment of these events leading up to World War Two in the opening article,"Those Distant Wars: Norwegian-American Attitudes Towards Poles and Finns, 1939-1940." Of course, the German occupation of Norway was of central importance to Norwegian Americans, and it loomed large over the actions and attitudes of Norwegian-American communities across the United States throughout the 1940s. Ann Legreid's piece "Campaigns on the Homefront: Norwegian-American Farmers and Workers Mobilized for War" offers an overview of the many activities Norwegian Americans engaged in to support both the United States and Norway during World War Two. Though the Midwest was a natural home to many of these activities, Norwegian Americans throughout the United States felt the consequences of the war. Hans-Petter Grav provides an in-depth analysis of how the war led Norwegian Americans in the Pacific Northwest to seek solace and purpose in their American and Norwegian identities in his contribution, "Our Values Are in Danger:

Norwegian-American Responses to World War II in the Pacific Northwest." The final article in the issue examines the postwar period. Siv Ringdal shows how the transatlantic flows of people, goods, and ideas prior to, during, and following the German occupation of Norway affected young, unmarried women migrants' experiences in "Dressing up in Post War America: Dreams, Experiences and Embodiment among Female, Norwegian Migrants in New York, 1945-1955."

These scholarly articles are framed by additional content related to the subject of war in the twentieth century. The Photograph Feature opens the issue by introducing us to the Camp Little Norway Club that was created in Chicago in 1941 to aid Norway's armed forces. In the Works in Progress, Kyle Ward and Odd Lovoll inform us of their book project on the 99th battalion - an ethnic Norwegian-American unit created by the United States military in World War Two. The volume concludes with our Notes from the Field, which highlights over 25 archival collections in the United States related to the subject of Norwegian Americans and war in the twentieth century. Each of these features reveals the breadth and depth of Norwegian-American involvement in the wars of the twentieth century.

My hope is that this issue will bring additional attention to the study of Norwegian-American life in the twentieth century. As evidenced in this volume, long into the post-World-War-Two period, Norwegian Americans felt a dual sense of connection to the United States and to Norway. War offers us a lens through which to view this subject as well as the entwined histories of gender, everyday life, identities, organizations, migration, ethnicity, and more.

—Anna M. Peterson, Associate Professor of History at Luther College

PHOTOGRAPH FEATURE

Camp Little Norway Club, Chicago

Deborah Miller

During World War II, many in Chicago's Norwegian community threw themselves into supporting the Norwegian war effort. To aid the Toronto-based Camp Little Norway, where Norwegian airmen trained for Norway's air force, forty-eight men organized the Camp Little Norway Club of Chicago (CLNCC) on November 3, 1941. Its aim was to collect gifts and funds for Norway's armed forces. Most of the members were what the secretary described as "Little Fellows—tradesmen and professional men and their families," so the dues were set at $1 a year.

The work of the Camp Little Norway Club of Chicago was divided between men's and women's efforts. The men organized fund drives and charity events, using meeting space at the Chicago Norske Klub at no charge. They sold stamps from the American Friends of Norway with pictures of a very young Prince Harald to help supply the Free Norwegian Fighting Forces with medical supplies. During

Figure 1. American and Norwegian flags followed the banner of the Camp Little Norway Club of Chicago as men, women, and children, some in Norwegian costumes, marched in Chicago's Seventeenth of May parade, ca. 1941–1944. From the Hermana Rye Haugan papers, 1906–1993 (P908). Courtesy of the Norwegian-American Historical Association, Northfield, Minnesota.

Figure 2. A cardboard membership card of the Camp Little Norway Club of Chicago includes the names of the club's president, financial secretary, and corresponding secretary in 1944, along with the name and address of the member. From the Hermana Rye Haugan papers, 1906–1993 (P908). Courtesy of the Norwegian-American Historical Association, Northfield, Minnesota.

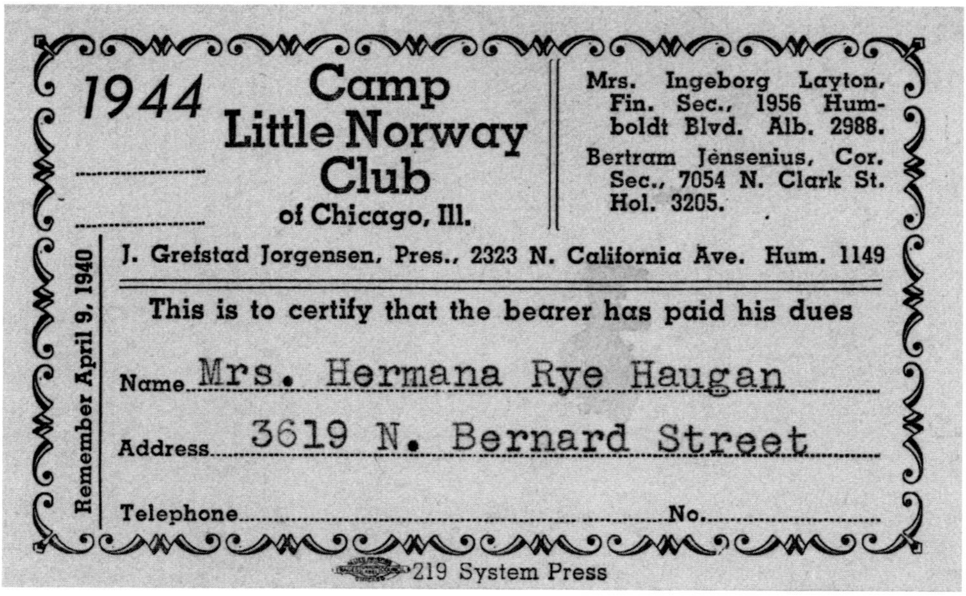

1944

Camp Little Norway Club of Chicago, Ill.

Mrs. Ingeborg Layton, Fin. Sec., 1956 Humboldt Blvd. Alb. 2988.
Bertram Jènsenius, Cor. Sec., 7054 N. Clark St. Hol. 3205.

J. Greistad Jorgensen, Pres., 2323 N. California Ave. Hum. 1149

Remember April 9, 1940

This is to certify that the bearer has paid his dues

Name Mrs. Hermana Rye Haugan

Address 3619 N. Bernard Street

Telephone .... No. ....

219 System Press

the five-year life of the club, they raised some $45,000 in cash to donate to the Norwegian cause.

The women helped supply the demand for knitting, especially wool socks, for the Norwegian armed forces. Some of the money raised by the men went to buy yarn for the women to use. Groups of women, including Daughters of Norway lodges, Ladies Aids, and the eleven women who informally organized Mina's Knitting Club, met in each others' homes to knit. At one point the knitters asked their leader, Hermana Rye Haugan, to inquire whether other woolen goods were needed along with socks, but the response from Olav Sørensen, welfare officer of the Royal Norwegian Air Force in Toronto, was clear: "Our continual need is socks." The CLNCC report in 1946, which summarized its history and accomplishments after it closed down, noted that Chicago women had knitted and sent the following items to Camp Little Norway: 205 sweaters, 1,477 pairs of socks, 67 pairs of wristlets, 160 scarves, and 75 chest warmers. The preferred stockings were Badger Socks No. 1019. The women also hosted fundraising events such as a talk by Sigrid Undset.

Figure 3. The American Friends of Norway pictured curly-haired Prince Harald, age 9, heir to the throne of Norway, on the victory stamps they sold to help purchase medical supplies for the Norwegian forces. From the Hermana Rye Haugan papers, 1906–1993 (P908). Courtesy of the Norwegian-American Historical Association, Northfield, Minnesota.

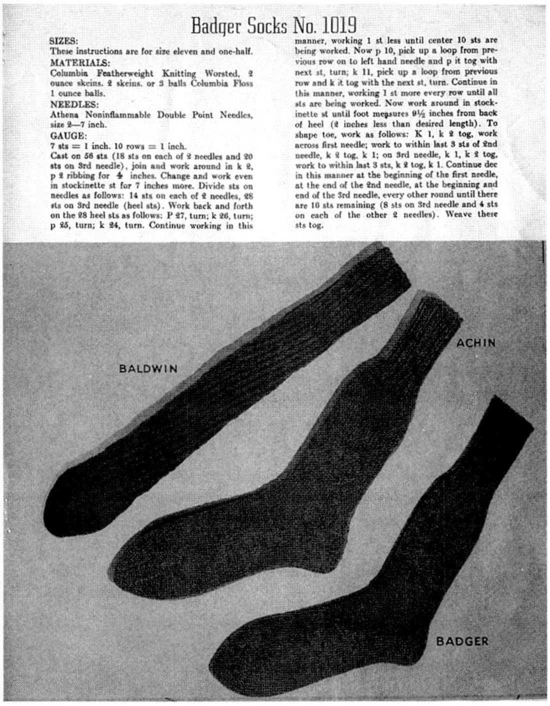

Badger Socks No. 1019

SIZES:
These instructions are for size eleven and one-half.
MATERIALS:
Columbia Featherweight Knitting Worsted, 2 ounce skeins. 2 skeins. or 3 balls Columbia Floss 1 ounce balls.
NEEDLES:
Athena Noninflammable Double Point Needles, size 2—7 inch.
GAUGE:
7 sts = 1 inch. 10 rows = 1 inch.
Cast on 56 sts (18 sts on each of 2 needles and 20 sts on 3rd needle), join and work around in k 2, p 2 ribbing for 4 inches. Change and work even in stockinette st for 7 inches more. Divide sts on needles as follows: 14 sts on each of 2 needles, 28 sts on 3rd needle (heel sts). Work back and forth on the 28 heel sts as follows: P 27, turn; k 26, turn; p 25, turn; k 24, turn. Continue working in this manner, working 1 st less until center 10 sts are being worked. Now p 10, pick up a loop from previous row on to left hand needle and p it tog with next st, turn; k 11, pick up a loop from previous row and k it tog with the next st, turn. Continue in this manner, working 1 st more every row until all sts are being worked. Now work around in stockinette st until foot measures 9½ inches from back of heel (2 inches less than desired length). To shape toe, work as follows: K 1, k 2 tog, work across first needle; work to within last 3 sts of 2nd needle, k 2 tog, k 1; on 3rd needle, k 1, k 2 tog, work to within last 3 sts, k 2 tog, k 1. Continue dec in this manner at the beginning of the first needle, at the end of the 2nd needle, at the beginning and end of the 3rd needle, every other round until there are 16 sts remaining (8 sts on 3rd needle and 4 sts on each of the other 2 needles). Weave these sts tog.

Figure 4. The pattern used by hundreds of Chicago's Norwegian women to knit socks for the airmen at Camp Little Norway. From the Hermana Rye Haugan papers, 1906–1993 (P908). Courtesy of the Norwegian-American Historical Association, Northfield, Minnesota.

After the war ended in 1945, Norwegian-American groups continued to organize aid to Norwegians in Norway, who were in great need of clothing, food, and other necessities. The CLNCC sustained its efforts into 1946. A larger Chicago women's group called Kle Norge Bua (Clothe Norway Shop) collected fifty thousand pounds of mostly used clothing to send to Norway, each piece of which had

Figure 5. Kle Norge Bua (Clothe Norway Shop) workers are pictured here in one of the empty stores rented for their work processing donated clothes for needy Norwegians after World War II. From the Hermana Rye Haugan papers, 1906–1993 (P908). Courtesy of the Norwegian-American Historical Association, Northfield, Minnesota.

to be sorted, repaired, cleaned, packed, and shipped. The value placed on the donated clothing was $150,000.

Records in the Norwegian-American Historical Association archives that document these efforts and more include the Hermana Rye Haugan papers, the Camp Little Norway-Chicago papers, and the Relief for Norway collection.

From the photos in these collections, it is clear that whenever Chicago Norwegians gathered during World War II, the Camp Little Norway Club was front and center, its banner visible in parades and celebrations.

Deborah Miller *is a public historian and retired reference specialist from the Minnesota Historical Society Library. She has an MA in Scandinavian Studies and serves as chair of the Norwegian-American Historical Association's archives committee. She hopes one day to find records of the Minneapolis-based head lodge of the Daughters of Norway.*

WORKS IN PROGRESS

The 99th Battalion

Kyle Ward and Odd S. Lovoll

Our forthcoming book, *Viking Battalion: The Norwegian-American's War against Hitler,* looks at the 99th Infantry Battalion (Separate), which was a unit made up specifically of Norwegian Americans and Norwegians in exile. While this unique unit would serve in Europe and be connected to some of the most famous battles and events in that theater of war, it quickly disappeared from the history books after the war ended.

The 99th was originally formed by the U.S. War Department in the summer of 1942. It was not the only "ethnic" unit the U.S. military tried to create during the war; others included the 100th (Japanese American), the 101st (Austrian American), and the 122nd (Greek American) Infantry Battalions. While the 101st and 122nd never really came to complete fruition, the 100th, along with its counterpart, the 442nd (made up of second-generation Japanese Americans), went on to receive a great deal of recognition for their service.

For their part, the 99ers were originally organized at Camp Ripley, Minnesota, and then sent down to Fort Snelling, Minnesota, for the first few months of

Figure 1. Men of the 99th during their training at Fort Snelling, Minnesota in the fall of 1942. After organizing at Camp Ripley, Minnesota, the 99th briefly trained at Fort Snelling before moving on to finish their training in Colorado. Author Kyle Ward's personal collection.

their existence. Then the army sent this group to Camp Hale, Colorado, to begin an extremely rigorous training regime in the high altitudes of the Rocky Mountains, where they were trained in mountain climbing, skiing, and winter survival.

During their training in Colorado, the 99th was reviewed by President Franklin D. Roosevelt, the commander-in-chief. A small part of our book will investigate this brief but highly publicized encounter. We believe that this small unit was highlighted by the president, and given a great deal of publicity, in order to send a message to Germany that the United States was preparing to invade Norway. If the

Figure 2. Two soldiers standing by a sign at Camp Hale, Colorado. The 99th would train at Camp Hale from December 1942 to August 1943, where they were put through some of the most strenuous training the U.S. Army had to offer. Author Kyle Ward's personal collection.

message was received and believed by Germany, Hitler would be forced to keep his 350,000 soldiers, plus their supporting planes, tanks, and ships, in Norway, rather than deploying them to other likely continental invasion sites, such as the Normandy region in France.

After training at Camp Hale, the 99th was sent to England and then, rather than going to Norway, actually landed on the Normandy beaches about two weeks after the initial invasion. From there, this relatively unknown group of highly-trained soldiers was sent across Europe, and participated in some of the most important and significant events in the European theater. A quick scan of their service record shows that they were at Cherbourg, held off SS attacks at the Battle of the Bulge, saved some of the survivors of the Malmedy massacre, guarded the gold and artwork found at Merkers Mine (depicted in the book and movie *Monuments Men*), and helped liberate the Buchenwald concentration camp.

Figure 3. Men of the 99th with medical training were part of the original group that helped liberate the German concentration camp at Buchenwald. Some of the men of the 99th are pictured along with recently liberated prisoners from the camp in April 1945. Author Kyle Ward's personal collection.

After the final surrender of Germany in May of 1945, the 99th was finally sent to Norway, where they were given the honor of serving as King Haakon VII's honor guard upon his return from exile. While the men were excited simply to finally get to Norway, some official duties remained, such as helping to remove the remaining German forces and working with Norwegian police and military to get them reestablished. On a more personal note, they also played a lot of soccer against Norwegian teams, spent time reconnecting with immediate or distant family, and for a few dozen, meeting their future wives.

Figure 4. Men of the 99th marching up from Karl Johan gate, Oslo, toward the royal palace, as part of a thank-you celebration for the allied nations that helped end the German occupation, summer 1945. Author Kyle Ward's personal collection.

Figure 5. At the royal palace, King Haakon VII addresses the men of the 99th and the crowd that gathered to celebrate the end of German occupation, summer 1945. Author Kyle Ward's personal collection.

Origins of the Project

Dr. Odd Lovoll (emeritus, St. Olaf) and I [Kyle Ward] met at a workshop that dealt with Norway and the Holocaust a few years ago. From that initial meeting the two of us have stayed in touch and continued our conversations about Norwegian history, Norwegian-American immigration, and more specifically, Norway during the Second World War. From those conversations we discovered that we both had an interest in the 99th Infantry Battalion. I currently serve on the 99th Infantry Battalion Educational Foundation board, and Dr. Lovoll has an even longer history of researching this group, even writing about them in his recently published memoirs, *Two Homelands.*

Given Dr. Lovoll's incredibly strong background in Norwegian and Norwegian-American history and my research and writing on military history, we decided about a year ago, after many conversations, to combine our interests and write a book about the 99th. Much of our work so far has centered on the idea that the 99th was composed of the last of the Norwegian Americans, meaning those descendants of the original immigrants who came to the United States and often held ties to their homeland. This group was used to adversity, hard work, and loyalty to two countries, qualities that would now meld to fight an enemy that threatened both of their homelands.

The Research and Writing Process

Our research so far has found that this unit was fairly typical of any group of Norwegian-American men of that time period. During the war they were not notorious for keeping journals, diaries, or writing a lot of letters home. Once the war was over, typically these men went back to their work and their lives and did not dwell on their exploits.

In our research, we have found a number of materials that have never been used before, as well as a few books and articles long overlooked by researchers. The following four books will form the backbone of this project. The first, Sharon Wells Wagner's *Red Wells: An American Soldier in World War II,* provides an interesting perspective because Wells joined the 99th as a replacement later on in the war, and was not Norwegian American. Next, two books were written immediately after the war, both published by the unit itself, which were mainly souvenirs for the soldiers and were both printed in Norway before the soldiers headed for home. One is titled *Company D: United States Army,* written by John W. Kelly, and the other is *History of the 99th Infantry Battalion,* written by Howard R. Bergen. Finally, the most famous book on the 99th was written by Gerd Nyquist, simply titled *The 99th Battalion.* Originally written in Norwegian, the work was translated into English and is currently sold through the 99th Battalion Educational Foundation. While it includes some analysis of her research, a large portion of the book is oral history as told by the soldiers of the 99th.

Among other materials we are coming across are a smattering of stories written down by soldiers or their families years after the war, a number of documents that the unit wrote during the war (especially a unit newspaper they published while in the United States and overseas), and materials gathered at unit reunions in the years following the war. Of utmost importance is a series of interviews collected in the 1990s by one of the children of a 99th veteran, who actually brought along a camcorder to some of the reunions and recorded interviews with a number of the men. An edited version of these was used for a documentary created by the Educational Foundation, but there are still many more hours unseen by the general public.

We are planning to do some research in Norway as well, to find more information about the time the 99th spent there, including Norwegians' reactions to the Americans, and more about the men who were not able to return home. Some of the locations we are considering are the National Archives (*Riksarkivet*), Oslo; the National Library (*Nasjonalbiblioteket*), Oslo; Norway's Home Front Museum (*Norges hjemmefrontmuseum*), Oslo; the Museum of Defense (*Forsvarets museum*), and the Narvik War Museum (*Narvik krigsmuseum*), Narvik.

Our goal is to complete our research and begin the actual writing by the summer of 2020. We anticipate a 2021 release date for the completed book. We are currently exploring the Minnesota Historical Society Press as a potential publisher.

Areas of Scholarly Engagement and Contributions

A New and Unique Perspective

Our project engages many historiographic discussions, including scholarship on Norwegian Americans, Norway in the Second World War, and ethnic units in the U.S. military during World War II. This topic offers a new and unique perspective. There have been literally thousands of books written about World War II from many perspectives, discussing contributions from individuals up to entire nations. Our research has shown that while the topic of World War II has been researched, analyzed, and written about countless times, we have uncovered a topic that is both relevant and unique, thanks to the interesting reason behind the 99th's creation, as well as their connections to a variety of events during the war. From a possible ploy in an international game of chess to fighting at some of the most famous battles in the European theater, this unit tells the story of World War II in a way few have ever heard before.

Norwegian Americans

Our book engages Gerd Nyquist's work and illuminates aspects of Norwegian-American life in the World War II era. Nyquist's book emphasized her belief that the 99th Infantry Battalion represented the last of the original Norwegian Americans. Our book will look at how there came to be such a large Norwegian-speaking group in the United States, why they clung to their culture and language, and why they settled where they did geographically. Two interesting side notes that our research has uncovered are as follows. First, one document shows that over 50 percent of the unit was made up of men from Minnesota or Brooklyn, New York. Second, when the army sent out a general call for soldiers who could speak a second language, a number of the original 99ers failed to respond, because, as one put it, he grew up speaking Norwegian at home, in school, and at church, and therefore never thought of Norwegian as a second language.

Ethnic Units

This research brings together the histories of Norwegian America and World War II, with a focus on one of the few ethnic units created in the United States. With the exception of the 100th and 442nd (the Japanese-American units), the story of the U.S. Army establishing specific ethnic units is a part of the World War II story that has gone largely unexplored by academics. This unusual concept, and the politics behind it, makes for an interesting twist relatively unknown to those interested in World War II. We hope to explore the reason these units were created and place them into the larger context by explaining why they were formed and what the U.S. military hoped to gain by creating such a unique grouping of soldiers.

Norwegian History

This work will also contribute to our understanding of Norwegian history during World War II and in the immediate postwar era. On April 9th, 1940, Germany invaded both Denmark and Norway, leading to the eventual conquest and occupation of both countries. The invasion not only forced Norway to enter the war, but also locked out a large number of Norwegian merchant mariners, who were unable to return to their families and homeland. Dr. Lovoll is intimately familiar with this situation, as this actually happened to his own father during the war. A great many of these men ended up in the United States, and when the call went out for soldiers who could speak Norwegian, they were ready and willing. Because Norway was occupied, the 99th gave these Norwegians the opportunity to serve in "their" own unit to help win the war.

Another topic we hope to explore is that, in at least one instance, a family had one son serving with the 99th, helping to defeat Hitler, while another son was in the SS, helping Germany fight the Russians. This illustrates a unique situation that Norwegians had to deal with during the war, in which they had to decide if they backed the Axis powers or the Allies.

Finally, there are a number of really great stories that deal with the 99th actually making it to Norway at the end of the war. They lead to a series of interesting connections for people interested in Norwegian history. For example, the 99th served as King Haakon VII's honor guard on his return to Norway and then helped parts of the Norwegian government re-establish itself following the war. On a more personal note, a great many of these soldiers were able to find the families they had left behind when they emigrated to the United States, families they probably had not seen in a number of years. Many descendants of immigrants to the United States were able to find grandparents and other relatives they had only heard about in the past.

***Kyle Ward** is Director of Social Studies Education and teaches history courses at Minnesota State University, Mankato. His doctoral dissertation researched how World War II has been portrayed in U.S. history textbooks and his first book,* In the Shadow of Glory, *dealt with a Minnesota National Guard unit during the Spanish-American and Philippine-American Wars. He currently sits on the board of directors for the 99th Battalion Educational Foundation.*

***Odd S. Lovoll** is a naturalized United States citizen. He received his education both in Norway and the United States, earning a PhD in U.S. History in 1973 with a specialization in immigration. He served thirty years on the faculty of St. Olaf College, retiring from the King Olav V Chair in Scandinavian-American Studies at the end of 2000. From 1996 to 2005 he served as adjunct professor (professor II) of history at the University of Oslo, and from 1980 to 2001 as NAHA's publications editor. His most recent book on the Norwegian-American immigrant experience, a memoir, carries the title* Two Homelands: A Historian Considers His Life and Work.

Those Distant Wars

NORWEGIAN-AMERICAN ATTITUDES TOWARD POLES AND FINNS, 1939–40

Terje M. Hasle Joranger and Daron W. Olson

Prelude to War

On Tuesday, July 11, 1939, a photo of Norwegian Crown Prince Olav and his wife, Crown Princess Märtha, aboard the ship *Stavangerfjord* in Brooklyn, New York, made the front page of the Norwegian-American newspaper *Decorah-Posten.* The royal couple were bidding goodbye to an enthusiastic crowd at the end of their successful ten-week visit to the United States.[1] In contrast, other news cast a dark shadow on the same front page, in an article titled "New Problems." These news items dealt with Germany and Japan and the threats that they represented in terms of political instability and a possible war. In a shorter article in the same issue, the newspaper reported that Germans in Gdańsk daily stated their determination to "return to the German Empire." From the Polish perspective, however, "Gdańsk was, is, and will always belong to Poland."[2]

This portentous juxtaposition on the eve of the Second World War was an ironic harbinger of the fate that would befall Norway. As the events of the early war years unfolded, people in the United States became distant observers of the tragic fate of small European nations who were at the mercy of large powers. Among American observers were Norwegian Americans, who could acquire information about the early war in Europe through newspapers in the United States. The Norwegian-American press wrote about the German invasion of Poland and

"DECORAH-POSTEN" HAS A LARGER CIRCULATION THAN ANY OTHER NORWEGIAN NEWSPAPER. Member Audit Bureau of Circulations. THE ANUNDSEN PUB. CO. Decorah, Iowa.

Decorah-Posten og Ved Arnen

No. 1. General Edition Decorah, Iowa, Tirsdag den 11te Juli 1939. General Edition

Nye Problemer.

Det norske Kronprinspars Hjemreise.

Kronprinsen udtaler en Tak og Hilsen til hele det amerikanske Folk.

Politisk Streik.

Mindegaven.

Danzig.

Landslærerforeningen.

Selveierpolitik.

Figure 1. The front page of Decorah-Posten, July 11, 1939. In the middle: Crown Prince Olav and his wife, Crown Princess Märtha, bidding goodbye to an enthusiastic crowd in Brooklyn at the end of their successful visit to the United States. To the left: An article titled "New Problems" discusses Germany and Japan.

the Winter War between Finland and the Soviet Union and brought the war actions on the European continent into their lives.

Several Norwegian-American newspapers, including *Decorah-Posten, Skandinaven, Nordisk Tidende,* and *Washington Posten,* were transnational in their outreach and strengthened ties that existed—or created new ties—between Norwegian Americans and their ancestral homeland.[3] As transnational newspapers, they had reporters and subscribers both in Norway and in the United States and, consequently, the newspapers made news available for a readership on both sides of the Atlantic. As indicated by the abundant presence of news about the Norwegian homeland in all the American Norwegian-language newspapers, readers were concerned about how world events impacted the land from which they and their ancestors had emigrated.

Although neither the invasion of Poland nor the Winter War between Finland and the Soviet Union directly involved Norway, urban and rural Norwegian-American newspapers presented these actions to their readers as highly relevant, taking positions that were sympathetic to the causes of Poland and Finland. Norwegian-American newspapers drew parallels between Poland, Finland, and Norway in an effort to cultivate sympathy among their readers, and at times call them to action. This aligned Norwegian-American newspapers closely to the larger body of American journalism. Both the American and Norwegian-American media depicted these wars as a larger struggle in which Poland and Finland represented the forces of Western civilization that were locked in a struggle with the forces of barbarism.

Attempting to place the reaction of Norwegian Americans and their viewpoints into a larger historiographical context is difficult owing to the limited studies on American wartime media coverage of the invasion of Poland and the Winter War. One study by Serge Cipko analyzes how the English-language presses of the Canadian province of Alberta affected Ukrainians there during the war. The coverage of the Poland campaign within the Alberta press led a pro-Soviet Ukrainian group to commit to supporting the British Commonwealth of Nations' efforts to defeat Germany, including an offer to raise a volunteer force of twenty-five thousand Ukrainian Canadians.[4] Of course, as a member of the British Commonwealth, Canada was already at war.

A study by Murray Katzman on American radio broadcasting stresses that radio network executives wanted to avoid offending both isolationists and interventionists in the United States. Yet he further observes that these radio broadcasts indicated that isolationism in America was dying in 1938 and that it was dead by the end of 1939. His insight suggests that the German invasion and partition of Poland with the Soviet Union, coupled with the Soviet invasion of Finland, meant that the American audience was highly sympathetic to the small nations of Europe as they battled against the Great Power dictatorships.[5] In a similar vein, Hideko Yoshimoto argues that media treatment (including newspapers) and government propaganda by the Roosevelt administration during this time created *anticipatory propaganda,* which led to the American perception that war might be necessary.[6]

In many ways, Norwegian-American newspaper coverage of the invasion of Poland and the Winter War was a part of this larger national media climate. Norwegian-American newspapers too presented Poland and Finland as small but mighty nations, and as bulwarks against extremism. Emphasizing the role of the gallant but tragic nations battling horrific odds, Norwegian-American newspapers highlighted similarities between Norway and Poland and Finland in order to make these events more personal to their readership, and thus more difficult to dismiss as irrelevant to their own lives. In doing so, the newspapers built a foundation from which they could not only cultivate sympathy but also move readers to act.

While the newspapers portrayed both Poland and Finland as worthy of sympathy, Finland received the bulk of attention. As a Nordic nation, Finland's geographic and cultural relationship to Norway was an easier case to make to readers. Numerous individuals and organizations responded to the newspaper coverage of the Winter War, involving themselves in relief efforts for Finland.

Historian Odd S. Lovoll argues that, thanks to the close ties between newspapers in Norway and the United States, the Norwegian-American press may be regarded as an extension of the press in Norway.[7] The press played a dual role by helping to create immigrant religious and secular organizations, and reinterpreted and reinvented the cultural traditions of their homeland to aid Norwegian

Americans in their creation of a new identity in the United States. Acting as a cultural bridge between the country of origin and the new society for Norwegian immigrants and their offspring, the Norwegian-American press nurtured this connection through their use of the familiar Norwegian language.

Many previous studies argue that rural Norwegian Americans were associated with localism in both the economic and social sphere, including an emphasis on family and kin, the neighborhood, and the local town and church.[8] A different perspective emerges when we consider Norwegian-American newspapers. Newspapers connected even the most isolated Norwegian Americans living in settlements far removed from the larger world. Certainly, Norwegian-American newspapers served to link Norwegian Americans to one another and to Norway. The newspapers also immersed them in distant places. When we examine the coverage of war actions in Europe, we can see how Norwegian-American newspapers not only strengthened Norwegian Americans' connections to Norway, they also engaged their readers in historical and cultural contexts far beyond Norway and the United States.

Scholars of Norwegian America have also been interested in exploring the dichotomy between rural and urban Norwegian-American culture.[9] Our analysis of urban and rural Norwegian-American newspaper coverage of the invasion of Poland and the Winter War contributes to this discussion. Of the three urban and five rural newspapers studied, urban newspapers tended to portray Poland the most sympathetically, often as a European fortress defending civilization against brutal and vicious forces. Still, the war in Finland had a much broader appeal to Norwegian-American readers than the war in Poland. All eight newspapers covered the Winter War much more extensively and enthusiastically than the war in Poland.

While these differences between rural and urban newspaper coverage are important to highlight, our examination of newspaper coverage of the invasion of Poland and the Winter War demonstrates that the urban/rural divide was less pronounced in connection with a sympathetic coverage of Finland and, to a lesser extent, Poland. This may be attributed to the fact that both rural and urban Norwegian-American newspapers were engaged in promoting the idea of a "greater Norway": a Norway that exceeded geographic and political boundaries to encompass Norwegians living abroad, especially in the United States.

In addition, the newspapers' positive and sympathetic portrayal of Finland and Poland may be connected to the adaptive process among Norwegian Americans in the United States attempting to become "good Americans." A continuous portrayal of events outside of Norway and the United States showed that Norwegian Americans were loyal and secure in their identity as Americans. Both urban and rural newspapers sided with two nations, Poland and Finland, that represented American values of liberty and democracy under attack by authoritarian regimes.

One might ask whether the coverage in these newspapers depended on the political leanings of their respective editorial staffs. During the heyday of Norwegian language usage in the United States, which was prior to World War I, this aspect would likely have been noticeable to readers. However, by the onset of World War II these papers were often the only Norwegian-language newspaper in their respective markets, so to avoid offending any particular segment of their readership, they tried not to stake out positions based on political orientation.

Norwegian-American Newspapers

Since the founding of the first Norwegian-language newspapers in the United States in the 1840s, the Norwegian-American press reflected the rise of an ethnic identity among Norwegian Americans. Based on shared national, religious, and cultural values, the ethnic press participated in community building among Norwegian Americans. By interacting with newspapers published in Norway, the ethnic Norwegian-American press kept the ties between a Norwegian-American population in the United States and Norway alive. The Norwegian-American press had seen a gradual decline in its readership during the 1930s, primarily due to the Great Depression, stronger demands for assimilation, and a declining Norwegian-born population. These three factors reduced ethnic distinctiveness among Norwegian Americans. In addition, the late 1930s and 1940s saw the discontinuation of Norwegian-American journals and the passing of significant individuals in Norwegian-American journalism. All told, these were signs that pointed toward the end of the great significance of the Norwegian-American press among Norwegian immigrants and their descendants in America.[10]

The celebratory visit of Norwegian Crown Prince Olav and Crown Princess Märtha to the United States in 1939 turned the tide for a certain period, as reports about their visit in the Norwegian-American press strengthened effective ties to nationality and heritage among its readership. Likewise, news about the outbreak of the Second World War, the German Nazi invasion of Norway on April 9, 1940, and the subsequent occupation of Norway until May 1945 resulted in a nationalistic fervor among Norwegian Americans. As a consequence, the Norwegian-American press experienced an ethnic revival during this period.[11]

This study examines coverage of the early months of the war through a comparison between five rural and three urban Norwegian-language newspapers. The rural papers are *Decorah-Posten* of Iowa, *Fergus Falls Ukeblad* of Minnesota, *Reform* of Eau Claire, Wisconsin, *Visergutten* of Canton, South Dakota, and *Grand Forks Skandinav* of North Dakota. The urban papers are *Skandinaven* of Chicago, *Nordisk Tidende* of New York, and *Washington Posten* of Seattle. These newspapers reveal the ways in which the Norwegian-American press responded to the German invasion of Poland in September of 1939 and the Winter War between Finland and the Soviet Union from November 1939 to March 1940 and how they presented these events to their readers.

We have examined all of these newspapers' coverage of both the German invasion of Poland and the Winter War in Finland, with the exception of some of the rural newspapers. Due to accessibility issues, *Decorah-Posten* is the only rural newspaper we have analyzed in terms of its coverage of both the war in Poland and the war in Finland. In addition, we chose to focus our attention on *Decorah-Posten* due to its importance. It had the largest circulation of any Norwegian-American newspaper and was by far the newspaper most widely read by rural Norwegian Americans.[12] The remaining four rural newspapers have only been analyzed for their coverage of the war in Finland, not in Poland.

All the rural newspapers were located in smaller cities and towns in the Upper Midwest, but in spite of their similar locations and common attachment to the Norwegian language they differed from one another to a significant degree in terms of number of subscribers, content, and political and religious allegiance. The largest of these newspapers, *Decorah-Posten,* was established in Decorah, Iowa, in 1874. Due to its national distribution, the newspaper was considered one of the Big Three, along with *Minneapolis Tidende* and Chicago's *Skandinaven,* and had a large number of subscribers both in America and throughout Norway.

Decorah-Posten appealed to a readership that identified with an older immigrant tradition in their appreciation for customs and traditions.[13] *Decorah-Posten* published a wide variety of content, from coverage of world news to local news in the United States and Norway, as well as serialized fiction. The newspaper, a semiweekly publication at the outbreak of the Second World War, attracted new subscribers with their use of subscription rewards and by publishing the popular cartoon *Han Ola og Han Per.*

The weekly *Fergus Falls Ukeblad* was established in west-central Minnesota in 1883. Originally, it supported the Farmers' Alliance and the People's Party and exerted influence in state elections, but following the defeat of the Populist Party in the 1890s the newspaper's circulation declined. The newspaper then assumed the role of an "independent reform paper," and it began focusing on local news from Otter Tail and surrounding counties and publishing announcements from the bygdelag movement. In the late 1930s, Marcus J. Quarum, born in North Dakota to Norwegian immigrant parents, moved to Fergus Falls and purchased the newspaper and its printing press. His ties to the Church of the Lutheran Brethren in Fergus Falls clearly influenced the *Fergus Falls Ukeblad.* The front page featured The Week's Sermon, and the newspaper regularly carried pious readings and temperance issues.[14]

Reform, a weekly published in Eau Claire, Wisconsin, was established in 1889. Waldemar Ager served as its editor from 1903, and the newspaper ceased publication with his death in 1941. Temperance was a significant cause for the Norwegian-American press around the turn of the twentieth century, and with its one-sided stance in defense of total abstinence and prohibition among Norwegians, *Reform* had a unique position among Norwegian-language temperance journals.[15]

Visergutten (The Errand Boy) was a weekly established in 1894 in Story City, Iowa, and succeeded a short-lived newspaper launched four years earlier. In 1917 publication was moved to Canton, South Dakota. In 1939 *Visergutten* was the only Norwegian-language newspaper in South Dakota, and, like *Decorah-Posten,* had subscribers in Norway and the United States. Unlike *Decorah-Posten*'s national distribution in both Norway and in the United States, *Visergutten* had a regional focus among subscribers in Norway. Its articles held news of contemporary Norway, with personal letters from its subscribers sharing joys and sorrows and letters to friends and kin making up a significant portion of the newspaper.[16]

Grand Forks Skandinav, a weekly, was established by Jørgen Fuhr from Trondenes near Harstad in 1927. He had organized the Fuhr Publishing and Printing Company in Duluth, Minnesota, nine years earlier. In 1933 another immigrant from Norway, Einar E. Fekjar from Valdres, purchased the newspaper and assumed the responsibility as editor. The newspaper had news from Norway as well as local coverage.[17]

The three urban newspapers in our study were located in Chicago, New York, and Seattle, all large cities with sizable populations of Norwegian immigrants and ethnic Norwegian Americans. Owing to demographic variables, they differed in their audiences and perspectives. Chicago was a Midwestern city and its heyday of Norwegian immigration occurred in the latter half of the nineteenth and the early twentieth centuries, so by the mid-twentieth century its Norwegian-American population was highly assimilated to American ways. New York's Norwegian immigrant population centered on the shipping industry, especially in Brooklyn, and its more international population often retained strong ties to Norway. Seattle, also a shipping center, had a more international Norwegian population than Chicago or the rural Norwegian settlements. In addition, the city had a later period of Norwegian immigration, beginning in the late nineteenth and early twentieth centuries. For these reasons, Seattle's Norwegian-American community had more recent ties to Norway, and a large number of its Norwegians were working class, therefore they viewed American society differently than the Norwegians of Chicago or New York.

John Anderson from Voss, Norway, launched *Skandinaven* in Chicago in 1866 while he was still head of the composing room of the *Chicago Tribune.*

He was one of the co-owners of *Skandinaven,* along with Iver Lawson (Ivar Larson Bøe) from Voss. Knud Langeland, longtime Norwegian-American journalist, assumed editorial responsibility. The paper was known for being anticlerical and pro-Republican party.[18]

Nordisk Tidende of New York made its first appearance in 1891. The Norwegian-American Seamen's Association provided the start-up capital to printer Emil Bernhard Nielsen. The newspaper's success relied on the loyal readership of native-born Norwegians who resided in the New York area, most of whom were involved in the shipping industry. As a result, its orientation differed from the Upper Midwestern Norwegian-American newspapers that relied on an immigrant population that was into its second and third generations.[19]

As for *Washington Posten,* it began publication on May 17, 1889, in Seattle in celebration of Norway's national holiday. Its founder, Frank Oleson, an immigrant from Trondheim, relied on reprinting material from Norwegian-American newspapers in the Midwest and eastern United States. Its focus was more communal and city-oriented than the large national Norwegian-language newspapers. The paper matured under the nurturing leadership of Gunnar Lund, who in 1905 assumed the twin roles of publisher and editor, making the paper into what Lovoll describes as "the Norwegian voice of the Pacific Northwest."[20]

These urban and rural Norwegian-language newspapers not only reported on issues related to Norway and Norwegian America, they also followed the political developments in Europe in the 1930s and interpreted them for their readers. The political issues in late summer of 1939 primarily centered around the Polish question following the German invasion in September, but quickly turned to the outbreak of war between Finland and the Soviet Union in November. Urban and rural Norwegian-American newspapers' treatment of these events reveal the varied ways in which they conceived of and articulated Norwegian Americans' relationships to Norway, Europe, and the United States.

The Norwegian-American press reflected the degree to which Norwegian Americans had assimilated to American life, including the degree to which they likely read more mainstream English-language newspapers in addition to the Norwegian-language newspapers. This may be attributed to the fact that

Norwegian Americans were privileged immigrants in the United States based on their racial credentials.[21] As a result, the process of becoming white was a way this immigrant group could position themselves favorably in the ethnoracial hierarchy of the United States as part of their identity and community building in their new homeland.[22]

Disaster in Eastern Europe

After the First World War, Poland was reestablished as an independent state for the first time since the Congress of Vienna in 1814–15. Thus, the future republic's territory had to be defined. Giving Poland access to the sea was one of the guarantees proposed by United States President Woodrow Wilson in his Fourteen Points of 1918. Poland acquired access to the sea through a strip of land referred to as the Polish Corridor or Danzig Corridor. The corridor, formerly part of West Prussia, divided the bulk of Germany from the province of East Prussia. The Free City of Danzig, now the Polish city of Gdańsk, was separate from both Poland and Germany. The following de-Germanization of the territory by Polish authorities in the 1920s and 1930s was met with increasingly revisionist policies after Adolf Hitler's rise to power in Germany in 1933.[23]

The aggressive foreign policy of Adolf Hitler's Germany threatened the carefully crafted balance of the Versailles peace treaty settlement, which in theory aimed to rein in the ambitions of the powerful nations of central and eastern Europe. The European world of the late 1930s was an uncertain and dangerous one for less powerful nations such as Poland. Following the Munich Agreement in October 1938, German minister of foreign affairs Joachim von Ribbentrop demanded the incorporation of the Free City into the Reich. On August 23, 1939, Nazi Germany and the Bolshevik Soviet Union signed a nonaggression pact, which provided a written guarantee that neither government would act aggressively toward the other or help an enemy of the other party. More importantly, the nonaggression treaty also included a secret protocol that defined the borders of Soviet and German "spheres of influence" in the event of possible rearrangement of the territories belonging to Poland, Lithuania, Latvia, Estonia, and Finland. When Germany and the Soviet Union signed their nonaggression pact it paved the way for

Figure 2. Comparison of planned and actual territorial changes caused by the Molotov–Ribbentrop pact. Courtesy of Wikimedia Commons.

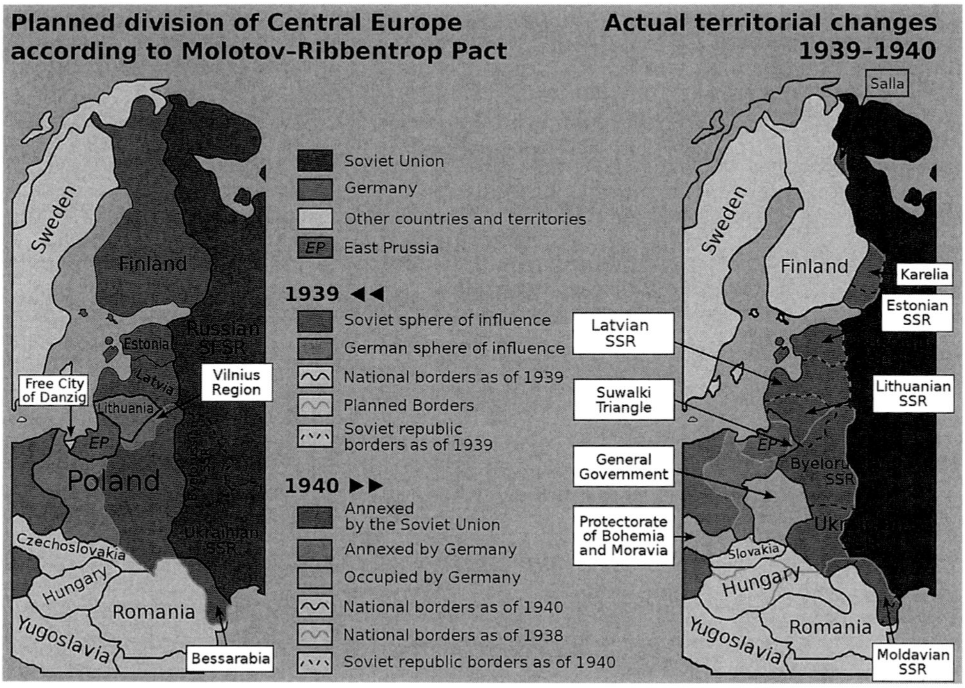

the future invasion and partition of Poland. Less than one month after signing the pact, Germany invaded Poland, on September 1, 1939. Two days later, Britain and France, both allies of the overrun nation, declared war on Germany. The initial stage of a new world war had begun.[24]

Of the three urban Norwegian-American papers, *Skandinaven* provided the most coverage of the plight of Poland by far. This situation is perhaps not surprising given the large Polish population of Chicago. The initial invasion on September 1, 1939, however, did not merit coverage. The first mention of Poland's situation was from September 12, nearly two weeks after the outbreak of the war. That day's editorial discussed Poland before and during the war's outbreak, noting that it had been a prosperous nation. Poland's population had increased by 30 percent to thirty million since 1919, while its industry had likewise grown, with exports becoming increasingly important. Poland's exports to the United States had shown significant growth. The editorial cautioned that what had happened to

Poland in terms of its invasion should raise alarm across the civilized world, for Poland's "independence has been violated." It expressed hope that the Franco-British alliance would help Poland achieve liberation.[25]

A few days later, on September 15, *Skandinaven* reported that German troops had isolated Poland's cities from the rest of the country. The article was optimistic in that the highest levels of command among the British and French would "give Poland the help of all their might."[26] A few days later, however, the situation looked bleaker as the paper observed that Germany had delivered its ultimatum for surrender and that the Polish government had fled to Romania. Many Polish troops joined the government there. *Skandinaven* observed that President Roosevelt had sent his sympathies for the German bombing of unarmed citizens in the cities and towns.[27] By September 26, *Skandinaven* reported that Poland had been divided between Germany and Russia. It quoted British prime minister Neville Chamberlain, who lauded the bravery of the Polish troops and criticized Hitler's description of the campaign as inaccurate and negative.[28]

Given time to reflect on the plight of Poland, *Skandinaven* published an editorial titled "Det ulykkelige Polen" (The unlucky Poland) on October 6, 1939. Making explicit parallels between Norway and Poland, the paper emphasized that Poland had become Christianized around the same time as Norway and "has since been a faithful daughter of the Roman-Catholic Church." It further noted the achievements of Poland, including progressive contributions by figures such as Copernicus, the father of modern astronomy, and the music of Chopin. It concluded that one had to go far back in history "to find a more brutal act of violence toward a noble, goodly, and freedom-loving people." In this depiction of Poland and its invasion, *Skandinaven* pinpointed an early theme of the war, namely that Poland represented the forces of democracy and freedom against the forces of barbarian aggression. This point of view became a hallmark of how Polish-American advocates for Poland depicted the basis of Poland's cause.[29]

Building on this sympathetic portrayal of Poland, the paper sought other ways to make Poland's invasion and the resulting war relevant to its Norwegian-American readership. On the same page as the editorial, the paper commented on the relationship between the Nordic lands and the newly declared war, reflecting on how the neutral Nordic lands were caught between Britain's ban on contraband and the German use of submarines. These opposing forces would likely severely reduce imports of foodstuffs to the Nordic nations. More importantly, Norway would likely see a diminution of its living standard and the Nordic lands' position was becoming more difficult and dangerous than it had been the during the First World War.[30]

Of the rural newspapers, *Decorah-Posten* had the most extensive news coverage of the outbreak of war in Poland. *Decorah-Posten*'s larger mission was to educate its readership about life in America and give its readers in America a sense of citizenship. When it came to the war in Europe, the newspaper also took on an educational role, and the news reports often explained the developments in Europe and presented the countries and key persons involved in a historical context. Yet, parallel to the educative reports of battles and advancing German forces in Poland and other world news, *Decorah-Posten* retained its contact with its readership on the local level. While the newspaper focused on the war in Poland and increasing tension in other parts of the world, various news columns reflected an impression of "business as usual" on the local level.

As a transnational newspaper, *Decorah-Posten* served as a bridge between the old country and the new land in that it formed a connection between a Norwegian-American readership in the United States and readers in Norway. The newspaper carried news columns from both Norway's rural communities and cities and various Norwegian strongholds in the Midwestern states, including columns about Decorah and vicinity and news from the Twin Cities. The newspaper also carried news from the bygdelag organizations, a column that discussed matters related to church and school, and entertained its traditional readers with local stories from the old days.[31]

Journalists in *Decorah-Posten* informed their readers of Germany's attack on Poland and the ensuing warfare as part of the newspaper's international news headlines and in editorials. It published news of the Danzig crisis on the front page of all of its semiweekly issues in July and August of 1939. Following the German invasion of Poland on September 1 and the British and French declaration of war two days later, editorials in *Decorah-Posten* covered the new developments. On September 5, for example, an editorial on the start of the war was titled "Ragnarok," referring to the apocalyptic final battle in Norse mythology.

During the war in Poland the newspaper included both the stance of the governments in the Nordic countries and of the United States government toward the war. Editorials sided with the Polish population but also supported the U.S. nonintervention policy. One editorial stated that "The U.S. President, Congress, [and] practically all Americans are against that the country enters the war. . . . We don't want to! All told, our people have learnt much from the war from '14 to '18 and still remember some of the bitter lessons. . . . A grown man doesn't need to beat others just to prove that he is a grown man."[32] When the war in Poland was over, a newspaper column stressed that America should keep the war at a distance and that extended trade between American countries was one of the best economic means of defense against a long war in Europe.[33]

While the editors felt it pertinent to inform Norwegian Americans of the developments in Poland, the readership of *Decorah-Posten* responded with limited engagement. In all the issues of *Decorah-Posten* during the war in Poland there is hardly any involvement from the subscribers. These issues only included a few letters to the editor about the warfare in Poland and there are practically no articles detailing any response from Norwegian-American institutions or organizations. The war was only mentioned by readers in conjunction with their own travel plans to Norway. For example, one of the newspaper's subscribers in Seattle noted in a letter to the *Decorah-Posten*,

> Quite many who had decided to travel to the Scandinavian countries will wait until the war planes have flown away, and must it happen quickly! Peace among all nations and peoples could be established in this moment if one wishes to use the means that the Lord himself has given, but as long as the warriors are fighting and people worship the Created instead of the Creator, who is blessed in all eternity, one can not expect anything else than sorrow, illness, and death.[34]

Observers in *Decorah-Posten* were most concerned with the practical consequences of warfare in Europe. In the column Alskens Nyt fra Tvillingbyerne (Various News from the Twin Cities) for example, the newspaper announced that the Sons of Norway's trip to Norway right after the international board meeting in New York next summer had been postponed because of the conditions in Europe. Final decisions about the trip would be taken by the end of the year.[35]

Photographs and columns in *Decorah-Posten* supplemented the tragic news about the war and portrayed it from various perspectives. A photo in the September 15 issue of the newspaper shows the U.S. ambassador to Poland, Anthony J. Drexel Biddle, and his wife stating that they left Warsaw with his staff while German bombers and artillery shelled the Polish capital. A bomb had hit the ambassador's residence while the family was at home, but no one was injured.[36] Another photograph in *Decorah-Posten* from September 19 had the title, "Korporal Adolf Hitler den tyske Hærs øverstkommanderende" (Corporal Adolf Hitler commander-in-chief of the German army).[37] In the column Rusk og Rask (Miscellaneous), readers of the *Decorah-Posten* ridiculed the German führer and his allies Italian dictator Benito Mussolini and Josef Stalin of the Soviet Union by referring to various war activities that had taken place.[38]

In the urban press, Hitler was likewise a favorite target. For *Washington Posten,* coverage of the Polish campaign often displayed biting sarcasm about Hitler's actions. Columnist Roald Lund observed on September 8 that "the Poles, by the way, are not Jews. But Hitler is finding they make just as good corpses."[39] In December, the paper lamented the fall of Warsaw, pointing to the many "old monuments, beautiful churches, and elegant castles." The latest conquest was the twelfth time the city had fallen to foreign invaders, highlighting a tragic side to Poland's history.[40]

Nordisk Tidende, out of New York, devoted slim coverage to the Polish campaign but did take umbrage with the impulsive words of famed Norwegian author Knut Hamsun. Writing the preface to a book on Danzig by Carl R. Fuchs, Hamsun termed the Poles a clever people who had earlier placed themselves in possession of Danzig, a German city in Germany. The author, who was noted for his fascist sympathies, believed the Poles had been "too clever" for thinking that they could cozy up to England as a way to take the city that properly belonged to Germany.[41]

As New York was home to a large Norwegian seamen's community, it is not surprising that *Nordisk Tidende* raised concerns about the safety of Norway's shipping industry. In an article from September 14, editor Carl Søyland wondered if the outbreak of the war meant that "if we sell our lives will we have anything to show for it?" He elaborated that Norway's merchant fleet faced an especially perilous situation and Norway's seamen faced potentially life-threatening situations on a recurring basis.[42]

On September 15, *Decorah-Posten* announced that the Germans were near Warsaw and that the United States Congress would get together six days later to discuss the situation. On September 19, the newspaper reported that a large Russian army had entered Poland; on September 29 *Decorah-Posten* announced Warsaw's surrender; on October 3 the newspaper carried Hitler's peace proposal.[43]

Concurrently, though less studied, the war in Poland and the later Winter War in Finland raised concerns among Norwegian Americans, many of whom worried about how aggressive militarism would affect the homeland of their ancestors. Following Poland's demise at the hands of its powerful neighbors, Finland would find itself embroiled in a difficult Winter War against the Soviet Union. The events in Poland and Finland raised concerns in the Nordic nations, including Norway and their compatriots in the United States.

The Winter War

The Nazi and Soviet Russian invasions left Poland devastated, but newspaper reports in various Norwegian-language papers in the Midwest soon turned their attention to Finland. A conflict erupted following Soviet claims to Finnish territory. The strategic and international position of Finland was largely altered as a consequence of the German-Soviet nonaggression pact. In the pact, the Soviet Union asserted a sphere of influence along its western border in the Baltic states and Finland. In early October of 1939 the government of the Soviet Union imposed stringent demands on the government in Helsinki. Russo-Finnish negotiations stalled because of the Russian demands, and on November 30, 1939, troops from the Soviet Union invaded Finland. Following the defeat of Poland a new war arena opened up in northeastern Europe; the Winter War had begun.[44]

As one might expect, coverage of Finland's Winter War against the Soviet Union prompted far greater coverage in Norwegian-American newspapers, likely because Finland was a Nordic nation. Even prior to the Soviet invasion, the Norwegian-American press expressed concern over Finland. Writing in October of 1939, columnist Lund of *Washington Posten* commented on how Norwegians and Swedes had traditionally not thought of Finns as Scandinavians, but the dangers of the war had changed everything. The Finns, he wrote, had become Scandinavians. Cooperation was the key to survival.[45] The sentiment carried over once the war broke out. In a December 5 editorial, *Skandinaven* denounced "the brutal aggression without provocation against the Finnish free state by the autocratic, power-hungry regime in Russia."[46]

The theme of a small Nordic nation battling against a Goliath-type neighbor resonated well in the Norwegian-American press. When Finland's ambassador to the United States, Hjalmar J. Procope, spoke to a Chicago audience in January 1940, *Skandinaven* emphasized that while Finland was not seeking direct aid from the neutral United States, "Finland was standing face-to-face with the Communist monster and operating under an ominous handicap."[47] These sentiments in the Norwegian-American press reflected the idea, also seen in the case of Poland, that Finland was fighting on behalf of democracy and Western civilization against the Asiatic hordes of the Soviet Union, an idea often promoted in the larger American press. For example, Dorothy Thompson, columnist for the *New York Herald Tribune,* used the following headline: "Stalin Detests the West: He Is an Asiatic."[48]

Early on, the outnumbered Finns achieved success against a Soviet army that had suffered from Stalin's purges of the 1930s. In early December for example, *Skandinaven* depicted the Finnish opposition which was making things difficult for Russia. The paper announced that Finland was holding its own against the Russian forces.[49] Around the same time, though, *Nordisk Tidende* acknowledged that "the Finnish folk was fighting for its existence" and urged its readers to send donations to Norway's Red Cross, which was giving much-needed aid to the Finns.[50]

The Winter War coverage in *Washington Posten* emphasized the shared vulnerability of the Nordic nations. Once again, Roald Lund observed that "Finland and the other Scandinavian nations are simply innocent bystanders and pawns in the war."[51] In the same issue from early December, E. J. Vickland invoked the "strong bonds" that for hundreds of years had tied Sweden and Finland together and proclaimed the Finns "our brother folk." The article, not surprisingly, ignored Sweden's domination of Finland, rather pointing to a sense of Nordic brotherhood in the difficult time of war.[52] Lund summed up this sentiment when he stated: "The group of small nations of Northern Europe known as the Oslo bloc has stood for one cardinal point: the right of the small nations to live peaceably and protect themselves through their union against the kiss of death of the warring powers."[53]

Beginning in 1931 the Nordic foreign ministers convened several meetings to discuss issues of common concern and security issues. In a joint declaration of neutrality from May 1938 they named and expressed the common ideals of the Nordic nations. Attempts to create a formal Nordic alliance, however, failed, owing to disagreements. A major problem was that Denmark viewed Germany as its primary threat while Finland viewed the Soviet Union as a supreme danger. The Norwegians, meanwhile, believed they would be left alone and that the British would save them, while Sweden preferred not to alienate the great powers. As such, the idea of a Nordic defensive pact to defend neutrality came up in meetings, but was never actually implemented due to lack of support.[54]

The early success of Finland against the Soviet Union led *Nordisk Tidende* to envision a united Nordic front against the invader. It observed in December how Finland's defense against the Soviet Union had been "capable and effective" and speculated whether the Nordic nations should openly join the war with Finland. Sweden, it noted, was the strongest and the richest and could raise a force of six hundred thousand. Norway, meanwhile, had the best navy of the Nordic nations, which could be a strong asset in the war. The paper also noted that Britain would likely not stand for Soviet interference in the Baltic and North Atlantic and would bring to bear its considerable naval and air power. Through combined action, it argued, the Kremlin would have newfound respect for the Nordic nations acting against a common foe.[55]

Norwegian-American newspapers reported the success of the Finns during the first months of the Russo-Finnish war, especially on the western side of the Karelian Isthmus and near Ladoga Lake. By early February the press reported that the Finnish army had destroyed Soviet Russian divisions, large amounts of military material, and taken thousands of prisoners.[56] Not until the end of February and early March did Norwegian-language newspapers shift their focus to Russian victories.[57]

When the war ended a few days later, the *Decorah-Posten*'s editorial stated that the Finns had gained the world's admiration and the attackers had gained the world's deepest contempt. The bloodbath had taken place in a war between two countries with uneven populations; 180 million against 4 million. As a result of

Figure 3. "Finland is fighting the cause of the entire Nordic region." Illustration from *Grand Forks Skandinav,* March 1, 1940.

the war, the editor noted, Finland had lost a large percentage of its youth and was economically in ruins. Viborg and other territories had become Russian, but Stalin forgot to "liberate" Finland as he promised. The editorial ended with a positive remark: "What is left of Finland is now free as it was earlier and will be governed by a democratically elected government."[58] Illustrations, often printed in Norwegian-American newspapers, also highlighted the fighting spirit of the Finns.[59]

Called to Action: Nordic Solidarity and Relief for Finland

The Russo-Finnish war created strong sentiments among countries that favored the Finnish cause. In contrast to the lack of enthusiasm over the war in Poland, both editorials and letters from readers expressed their strong support of the Finnish cause in the Norwegian-language press. As the Winter War progressed, the Norwegian-American press became alarmed that Norway might be next. In *Washington Posten,* columnist Lund expressed that at one time there had been hope for the Soviet Union as it had been a champion of collective security. In fact, during the 1930s, the Soviet Union under Stalin consistently supported collective security as a deterrent to the aggressive ambitions of the Nazi regime.[60] Yet, he confessed that "faith in the infallibility of Stalin" made such hope untenable. He decried Soviet attempts to paint Finland in a negative light: "No criticism of Finland, no rationalization on behalf of the Russian cause, can quite make us forget that Sweden follows Finland and over Kjölen lies Norway."[61]

As late as January the Norwegian-American Press saw moments of hope. *Skandinaven* reminded its readers that Finland was making a stand, but desperately needed additional aid.[62] A couple of weeks later, *Nordisk Tidende* issued a more dire warning, stating that "it was the eleventh hour" for Finland, which was "fighting for its freedom and independence." It noted that outside sympathy and moral support gave strength to the Finnish soldiers, but they could not hold out forever against the Russian hordes. And it asked, "If Finland falls, what would happen to the rest of Scandinavia?"[63]

Moments of Nordic solidarity lifted the spirits of Norwegian-American readers. In early February, *Nordisk Tidende* printed a picture of smiling volunteers from Norway who had gone to Finland to fight against the Soviet forces. The paper reported that thousands of Norwegian volunteers between the ages of seventeen and thirty-three had freely traveled to Finland,[64] a strong gesture of Nordic brotherhood.

For Norwegian-American readers, however, the emotional roller coaster continued. Following weeks of bad reports and Soviet victories, *Skandinaven* could finally report on February 16, 1940, that Finnish victories were still occurring

NORWEGIAN NEWS NORSKE NYHETER

Torsdag den 8. Februar 1940

Smilet dekker Norges Alvor mens Øiet vendes østover

Sangernes 50 Aars Konsert 18. Februar

Spionasje Forsøk i Oslo?

Tre Skiklubber støtter Fondet for Finnene

Figure 4. Norwegian volunteers headed for Finland. From *Nordisk Tidende,* February 8, 1940.

as the famed Mannerheim Line held. But the paper mentioned that Finland could use immediate relief.[65]

Late in the war during March, *Washington Posten* called out to its readers with a headline that read "Finland Needs Help." Beneath the caption appeared a drawing showing Soviet planes bombing a cabin in the woods as a fleeing Finnish mother holds her baby tightly. The article indicated that the Norwegian-American chapter of the Finnish Relief Fund out of New York had taken the initiative to raise more funds.[66] The drawing obviously played to the emotional sympathies of Norwegian readers.

Figure 5. "Finland Needs Help." Illustration from *Washington Posten* March 8, 1940.

Yet despite the brave fighting spirit of the Finnish soldiers, the outcome of the war hung like a fatalistic vision of the Ragnarok referenced earlier in *Decorah-Posten* in regards to the invasion of Poland. Late in February, *Nordisk Tidende* ran a *New York Times* article titled "Salute to the Brave," in which it began: "For seventy-one days the Finnish Army, fighting with its back to the wall, has staved of [sic] the inevitable." The article elaborated that there was never any reason to believe that a nation of a few million people could prevail against an adversary many times its size. The *Times* credited the Finns for their class, noting that "To the cheap taunts and vicious slander of the Kremlin they have replied with dignity." The article concluded by claiming that "Finland will remain a living symbol and a present influence on the affairs of men as long as liberty is cherished."[67]

Skandinaven, meanwhile, called for Finland to receive massive material aid, which might give her a fighting chance. In an editorial from late in February, the paper observed that Finland had recently called up men in their forties to fight. It advised the other European powers, likely meaning Britain and France, to provide Finland with good quantities of weapons of all kinds and urged that the best path for material aid would be over the northern way through Norway and Sweden.[68] This plan faltered, however, and only one British brigade actually set foot on Finnish soil. However, the threat of a stronger Allied invasion likely deterred the Soviet Union from conquering Finland at the time, since the Soviet government considered Norway and Denmark to be in the British sphere of influence and conquering Finland would threaten the balance.[69] These appeals had little chance, of course, and by the ides of March *Skandinaven* dutifully reported that the Russian-Finnish campaign was over. Its article lavished praise on the Finnish troops, describing them as "having gone farther at holding out during the campaign than would have been expected."[70]

The sense that Finland had been abandoned in military terms by its allies became an issue shortly thereafter when its Nordic neighbors emphasized their humanitarian aid to the defeated nation. Responding to the charge that a military relief force of thirty thousand had failed to sail to Finland owing to resistance from Norway and Sweden, E. J. Vickner, writing in *Washington Posten,* argued instead that Norway and Sweden had been strong supporters of Nordic neutrality and would not have stood in the way of such relief to their beleaguered neighbor. He was especially adamant that Sweden "had never opposed aid to Finland."[71] In fact, Britain and France had in early February agreed on a plan to send one hundred fifty thousand troops to conquer the ice-free port of Narvik, Norway, and then march into northern Sweden to occupy that country's iron mines. Lastly, the Allies would march into Finland to fight the Soviets. According to British prime minister Neville Chamberlain the goal was to "kill two birds with one stone."[72]

British and French sources had criticized Norway's unwillingness to allow the military aid to pass on its way to Finland, a charge that some American sources had likewise echoed. *Nordisk Tidende* printed a strong rebuttal in late March:

> It is so easy to criticize, especially when one sits several thousand miles away. But Norway lies geographically anchored to the European danger zone and understands these realities. We have said it before and say it again now: Norway itself knows what the country and people are best served by. Therefore, let Norway take the decision and trust in its best judgement.[73]

In reality, the decision not to invade via Norway came down to Finland, and the Finnish government, led by the war cabinet of Risto Ryti, refused to make a formal public request for help. Finland did want to risk alienating its Nordic neighbors and losing control of its own fate, becoming a pawn in a greater power struggle. The Finns also had doubts about the Allied plan since the plans changed so often.[74]

Norwegian-language newspapers called their readers to action. In February 1940 a *Decorah-Posten* subscriber from Bagley, Minnesota, wrote that he supported American private contributions to Finland with money etc. as they were doing in the Scandinavian countries. Another man wrote in *Reform* that he was happy to give relief to Finland as a means to help Norway and the Nordic region.[75] Another reader from *Decorah-Posten* in Viroqua, Wisconsin, wrote the following:

> [The Finns], a free people who does not do anyone any harm, is to be crushed by the bloodthirsty devil Stalin. We pray for Finland,

> that God will help the people, that the Russian Bear is not allowed to exterminate them. . . . It is a blessing that the whole world has sympathy for Finland and may anyone who can help these poor people.[76]

Such optimism proved short-lived, however, as the Soviet Union brought its superior numbers to bear in the war. A *Nordisk Tidende* editorial from early January memorialized "the dead in the snow," a reference to the corpses of "our Finnish friends."[77] Often relief for Finland was portrayed as support for Norway. In January of 1940 a journalist in *Fergus Falls Ukeblad* stated the following:

> The relief that can be sent from America to Finland is indirectly relief to Norway. It is no secret that the Soviet Union is directing its eyes at Norway and it is therefore of historical importance to do our utmost to keep the Russians east of the Finnish lines. Norwegian Americans are well organized in the U.S.A., and they have never failed in the darkest hour.[78]

In early March, the editorial in *Decorah-Posten* stated that "swift relief was needed for the courageous Finns who fought against Russian predominance. . . . Although Finland receives support and relief from Scandinavia and other European countries and also Americans and many volunteers," the editor noted, "[we believe that] all peoples of Europe suffer under the burden of war between great powers. Therefore, we believe that big, neutral America must help with all means so that Finland can be saved from extinction."[79]

By that time, the United States had responded to this call to help the Finns, and former president Herbert Hoover was a central figure in this respect. In December 1939 *Decorah-Posten* announced that Herbert Hoover had established a national organization, the Finnish Relief Fund, Inc., with headquarters in New York.[80] He took leadership in collecting voluntary contributions to support the needy in Finland because of the war.[81] The money collected for the Finnish Relief Fund was to go to the reconstruction of the war-stricken Finnish Republic, and Scandinavian Americans could continue to do their part by contributing to the fund. In mid-January Herbert Hoover appointed a committee for the American Norwegian division of Finnish Relief Fund, Inc.[82] The division in turn had district committees spread all over the United States.[83] In other words, the support was initiated on the national level and soon spread through various organizations to include fundraising on the local level.

In late December of 1939 Herbert Hoover, as chairman of the Finnish Relief Fund, had spoken in Minneapolis to a crowd of eight thousand people. In January 1940, *Decorah-Posten* announced that the Minneapolis committee for relief to the needy in Finland had sent more than $18,000 to the main committee in New York.[84]

The fraternal organization Sons of Norway International responded to the call and played an active role in collecting money for the relief fund.[85] In late December of 1939 *Fergus Falls Ukeblad* reported that the international board of the Sons of Norway had sent an appeal to Norwegians in America to aid "the unfortunate Finnish people." The article included the following message: "Everyone knows what it is all about. One of the free Nordic peoples is threatened with annihilation. The entire fate of the Nordic region is at stake. . . . We can at least participate in lessening the need among war casualties."[86] The relief for the Finns coordinated by the Sons of Norway was to be sent through the Norwegian Red Cross, and the organization asked lodges, organizations, and individuals to collect money in each district to send to the Sons of Norway's headquarters in Minneapolis.[87] In this manner relief work spread to numerous Sons of Norway lodges in the United States.[88]

In February the newspaper *Reform* announced that contributions to the Finnish Relief Fund had come from all over the United States as a result of the nationwide campaign for the Finnish civilian population. For example, the chairman of the Norwegian-American division of the Finnish Relief Fund had sent an appeal to 280 ski clubs in the United States and asked them to set aside part of the income from ski tournaments for the collection of funds. In addition, four hundred yacht clubs in the U.S. mainland and Honolulu had been asked to contribute to the division. Prominent speakers from Scandinavia had toured the United

States in support of the relief work. The board of the Brooklyn Norsemen Ski Club, the oldest organization of winter sports on the East Coast, made a decision to provide 10 percent of income generated from large events to the relief fund. In Helena, Montana, and Sioux Falls, South Dakota, committees were established to aid in the collection of money for the Finnish Relief Fund. Norwegian Lutheran pastors in Brooklyn, New York, and prominent Norwegian Americans in New Haven, Connecticut, also established relief committees.[89] Local politicians also did their part in organizing aid to the war-stricken Finns.[90]

Ethnic cultural organizations participated in the collection of funds as well. In early March 1940, for example, *Decorah-Posten* carried the news that representatives from the Decorah chamber of commerce, *Det norske Selskab* (The Norwegian Society), the literary society *Symra,* and other organizations in Decorah, Iowa, and the surrounding area had created Winneshiek County Finnish Relief. Later that month the *Totenlaget* in Minneapolis was to hold a festive event at Bethel Lutheran Church, Minneapolis, where the income was to benefit the Finns.[91] Various other sources of income were also introduced.[92] In early March of 1940 prominent Scandinavian Americans in New York City took on a more activist stance and joined an organization called "Fighting-Funds for Finnland [sic], Inc."[93]

A sense of urgency likewise defined the attitudes of the urban Norwegian newspapers. *Skandinaven* of Chicago promoted continued relief for Finland and in an editorial, the paper observed that Russian camps held two hundred thousand Finnish troops while approximately four hundred thousand Finnish women and children required immediate assistance owing to harsh conditions in Finland. To meet these needs would require generous giving as the Red Cross reported that it needed $400,000.[94] Roald Lund of *Washington Posten* published similar remonstrations. He urged Norwegian Americans to continue to contribute to aid for Finland, which was needed more than ever with the war's conclusion. He also used the occasion to exclaim that "the Norwegian nation has been a champion of lost causes." He elaborated further: "That obstinate clinging to and supporting of an ideal is a Norwegian characteristic that has hardly washed out of the Norwegian-American people. And it is up to them and the other Scandinavian Americans now.

For with the ending of the war, the spirit will naturally go out of the general campaign for funds."[95]

On March 15, 1940, the press reported that the Finnish-Russian war had ended two days earlier.[96] A few weeks after the end of the Finnish-Russian war, chairman of the Finnish Relief Fund, Herbert Hoover, declared that Finland needed the support from the outside world more than ever. He mentioned that the Scandinavian nations had offered their generous support from the beginning, and he called Americans of Scandinavian descent to do their utmost to help the Finnish people reconstruct their country.[97] However, one month later, three days after the German invasion of Norway, *Decorah-Posten* announced that the newspaper had put aside letters from subscribers regarding the situation in Finland "as they will not serve their intended purpose."[98]

Conclusion

The Norwegian-American press reflected various responses to the two arenas of war in Europe in the fall of 1939 and the winter of 1939 to 1940. This difference owed a lot to the perceived distance—both literal and emotional—that Norwegian Americans felt for Poland and Finland respectively. Through their newspapers, Norwegian Americans revealed sympathy for Poland, but the nation was in many ways distant owing to its location on the European continent and not intimately connected to Scandinavia. Finland, however, was different, and Norwegian Americans considered her a fellow Scandinavian nation whose fate was portentous for the potential wartime fate of Norway.

Decorah-Posten and three major urban Norwegian-American newspapers had a varied response to the war in Poland and approached it differently than they did Finland. The German Nazi and Soviet Russian attack on Poland was portrayed from a distance in editorials and as part of the world news but without any involvement on the organizational or individual level among Norwegian Americans. *Skandinaven* had the most coverage of Poland and it centered on empathy for the unlucky Poles who as a small nation faced insurmountable odds at the hands of their powerful adversaries. *Washington Posten* offered similar coverage, albeit focused on the tragic side of Poland's history, of which World War II was the latest chapter. *Nordisk Tidende* offered the scantest coverage and oriented its coverage to how developments in Poland would likely impact Norway. In one sense, though, the urban Norwegian-American newspapers, particularly *Skandinaven* and *Washington Posten,* shared in a larger American media trend of depicting Poland as a bastion of Western civilization in battle with the forces of barbarism. While these direct parallels with the larger American press were missing in *Decorah-Posten* and *Nordisk Tidende,* their presence in the other two papers suggests that at least some Norwegian Americans had sympathy for Poland, albeit on a more conceptual level than for Finland.

Journalists for the rural newspapers *Decorah-Posten* of Iowa, *Fergus Falls Ukeblad* of Minnesota, *Reform* of Wisconsin, *Visergutten* of South Dakota, and *Grand Forks Skandinav* of North Dakota provided detailed information about warfare in distant countries in Europe to their readership. Although their approach differed, these rural newspapers connected Norwegian-American communities to the German Nazi invasion of Poland and the Winter War between Finland and the Soviet Union. In this manner, the readership of these newspapers was exposed to content that differed significantly from traditional news columns in the respective newspapers. These rural newspapers also provided their readership with detailed information about an ongoing crisis. More importantly, the news reports gave an impetus for readers to engage actively in the relief work for the Winter War in Finland.

The portrayal of the Winter War in Finland was treated by both rural and urban newspapers in a more empathic and enthusiastic manner than the news coverage of the war in Poland. Whereas the Norwegian-language press supported the Polish government and its population in their hardships, the support never became as deep as it was with Finland. Editorials and letters from subscribers and the local efforts of nonprofit organizations revealed strong support for the Finnish population. All eight newspapers tended to converge as the reality of a difficult campaign so close to Scandinavia struck home. The brave fighting Finns far exceeded expectations yet there was a sense of fatalism about the war, the sense that Finland could not hold out indefinitely against its menacing neighbor. The newspapers all urged their readers to give generously to relief for Finland, seeing the vulnerability of the Finns as a parallel to the vulnerability of Norway.

The Norwegian-American papers also displayed grave concern that the war might spill into Norway with similar and predictable results. For example, in February 1940 Roald Lund of *Washington Posten* argued that relief aid was merely "fattening Finland for the slaughter" and instead he advocated that the United States immediately provide weapons and real assistance.[99] Back in October of 1939, Lund had wondered how the identity of the Scandinavian nations would fare "in the noisy and highly unpleasant wild west poker game in Europe."[100]

As revealed in the Norwegian-language press, Norwegian-American attitudes—especially when one considers the coverage of Finland and the Winter War—skewed toward an interpretation in which the bravery of Finland and, to a lesser extent, Poland, indicated that the war in Europe was increasingly about a battle between civilized democratic nations and their more powerful but uncivilized neighbors, namely Nazi Germany and Communist Russia. Thus, the Norwegian-American viewpoint on the war converged with that of the larger body of American journalism, which Karen Dearlove observes depicted the wars in Europe as a confrontation between Western civilization and Eastern barbarism.[101]

Norwegian-American newspaper coverage of these distant wars, along with their readers' corresponding intellectual and financial engagement, runs counter to the portrayal of Norwegian Americans as living in a relatively secluded sphere centered on local community building.[102] Norwegian Americans associated an attack on Finland with an attack on Norway and, consequently, on themselves. The resulting empathy and activity among the Norwegian-American population to help Finland reflected feelings of solidarity with a peaceful, brotherly people. In spite of a strong commitment to the Finnish cause, the Winter War in Finland raised the ominous prospect that World War II might soon engulf Norway. The Winter War and Finland's fate revealed that the stakes were indeed high—and most deadly—a lesson proven on April 9, 1940, when a new chapter of the Second World War began.

Terje Mikael Hasle Joranger *is director of the Norwegian Emigrant Museum near Hamar, Norway. He earned his PhD at the University of Oslo in 2008 and is co-editor of* Nordic Whiteness and Migration to the USA: A Historical Exploration of Identity *(Abingdon and New York: Routledge, 2020). He also has published several articles on migration and ethnicity in national and international publications. He is editor of* Norwegian-American Essays *and former chair of NAHA-Norway.*

Daron W. Olson *is Associate Professor of History at Indiana University East, where he teaches European and World History. He is the author of* Vikings across the Atlantic: Emigration and the Building of a Greater Norway, 1860–1945 *(University of Minnesota Press, 2013) as well as numerous articles on Norwegian immigration.*

NOTES

1. "Det norske Kronprinspars Hjemreise," *Decorah-Posten* July 11, 1939. Several Norwegian-language and English-language newspapers in the United States had news about the visit of Norwegian Crown Prince Olav and Crown Princess Märtha in the spring and summer of 1939. See for example reports in *Scandia American Scandinavian News* (Chicago), May 4, 1939; "St. Olaf Acclaims Olav and Martha," *Northfield News* (Minn.), May 11, 1939; "Program: Visit of H.R.H. Crown Prince Olav to Alexandria, Minnesota, Saturday, June 10, 1939," *Fergus Falls Ukeblad,* May 17, 1939; "Stor Begeistring For Kronprinsparets Besøk," special issue of the *Grand Forks Skandinav,* June 2, 1939; "Souvenir Edition in Honor of Crown Prince Olav and Crown Princess Martha's Visit to South Dakota," *Visergutten* June 14, 1939.
2. All translations are by the authors. "Danzig," *Decorah-Posten,* July 11, 1939. Gdańsk or Danzig was technically a free city set up by the League of Nations, but because the League had detached it from Germany it remained a symbol of national embarrassment for many Germans. See https: //encyclopedia.ushmm.org/content/en/article/danzig.
3. During the period from 1925 to 1939, transnational celebrations involving both Norway and Norwegian America remained popular and they indicated the bonds felt by Norwegian Americans toward their ancestral homeland. See Daron W. Olson, "On Both Sides of the Atlantic: Transnational Celebrations of Norwegian National Identity, 1925–1939," *Norwegian-American Studies 2014* (Oslo: Norwegian-American Historical Association–Norway and Novus Press, 2014), 118–20.
4. Serge Cipko, "The Alberta Press on Ukrainians in Canada during World War II: Two Case Studies," *Canadian Ethnic Studies* 47:4–5 (2015) [French edition 42:2–3 (2010)]: 291.
5. Murray Katzman, "News Broadcasting in the United States, 1920–1941" (PhD diss., New York University, 1968), 290–91.
6. Hideko Yoshimoto, "Media Treatment of World War II in Japan and the United States, 1931–1945" (master's thesis, San Jose State University, 1994), 65.
7. Odd S. Lovoll, *Norwegian Newspapers in America: Connecting Norway and the New Land* (St. Paul: Minnesota Historical Society Press, 2010).
8. Lori Ann Lahlum, "Women, Work, and Community in Rural Norwegian America,

1840–1920," in *Norwegian American Women: Migration, Communities, and Identities,* eds. Betty Ann Bergland and Lori Ann Lahlum (St. Paul, 2011), 84–95; C. Ostergren, "European Settlement and Ethnicity on the Agricultural Frontiers of South Dakota," *South Dakota History* 13:183 (1983): 49–82; Terje Mikael Hasle Joranger, "The Migration of Tradition? A Study on the Transfer of Traditions Tied to Intergenerational Land Transfers among Emigrants from the Valdres Region, Norway, to the Upper Midwest and Their Descendants for Three Generations, 1850–1980" (PhD diss., University of Oslo, 2008).

9. Lovoll, *Norwegian Newspapers,* 3–5; Terje Mikael Hasle Joranger, "Lokale eller nasjonale kollektive identiteter? Etnifisering og identitetsbygging blant norske immigranter i Amerika," *Historisk Tidsskrift* 89:2 (2010): 232–37.
10. Lovoll, *Norwegian Newspapers,* 204–5, 301–2, 319, 325.
11. Lovoll, *Norwegian Newspapers,* 310, 319–21.
12. Lovoll, *Norwegian Newspapers,* 216–17.
13. *Decorah-Posten* served as a weekly paper from its beginnings in 1872 to 1897. It then became a semiweekly newspaper but saw a shift to weekly issues from 1941 until it ceased publishing in 1972. By 1924, the number of subscribers abroad, not counting Canada, was 1,183. In 1939 it included the *Minneapolis Tidende* in its fifty-third year, a continuation of *Nordvesten* (fifty-ninth year), *Budstikken* (sixty-seventh), and *Emigranten* (eighty-eighth year). Lovoll, *Norwegian Newspapers,* 211, 216, 272, 279–80, 355.
14. The newspaper was established as *Fergus Falls Ugeblad,* but from 1938 the spelling was changed to *Fergus Falls Ukeblad.* Consequently, the latter spelling has been used in this article. The newspaper ceased publication in 1946. The Bygdelagenes Fellesraad website defines "bygdelag" in the following manner: "Bygdelag are organizations comprised of descendants of emigrants from Norway to North America. Every 'Lag' seeks to preserve and strengthen bonds with its home district or community-of-origin in Norway." Lovoll, *Norwegian Newspapers,* 119–22, 237, 327–28, 358; Norwegian-American Bygdelagenes Fellesraad [cited May 1, 2019]. Online: http: //www.fellesraad.com/fell_about.htm#bygdelag.
15. Lovoll, *Norwegian Newspapers,* 237, 242–45, 369.
16. *Visergutten* continued operation in Canton, South Dakota, until 1944 when it was moved to Fargo, North Dakota. It was in operation until 1955. Lovoll, *Norwegian Newspapers,* 155–58, 217, 314, 356.
17. Lovoll, *Norwegian Newspapers,* 280, 315–17, 365.
18. Lovoll, *Norwegian Newspapers,* 74–76.
19. Lovoll, *Norwegian Newspapers,* 199, 288–89.
20. Lovoll, *Norwegian Newspapers,* 190–93.
21. Like other immigrant groups in the United States, Norwegian immigrants achieved their status as white by demonizing others. This tendency is noted by many immigrant scholars, including David Roediger, Mathew Fry Jacobson, and James Barrett. See Victoria C. Hattam, "Whiteness: Theorizing Race, Eliding Ethnicity," *International Labor and Working-Class History* 60 (Fall 2001): 64–65.
22. As a social construct, race has not always meant the description of biological differences but could be used to describe other cultural groups and nations and vary across time. See Erika K. Jackson, Jana Sverdljuk, Terje Mikael Hasle Joranger, and Peter Kivisto, eds., *Nordic Whiteness and Migration to the USA: A Historical Exploration of Identity* (Abingdon

and New York: Routledge, 2020); Monika Žagar, *Knut Hamsun: The Dark Side of Literary Brilliance* (Seattle, University of Washington Press, 2009): 132–33.

23. Antony Beevor, *Den andre verdenskrig* (Oslo, 2012), 32–33; Richard Overy, *1939: Nedtelling til krig* (Fagernes, 2009), 11–31.
24. Beevor, *Den andre verdenskrig,* 33–34, 42–44.
25. "Polen for og ved Krigens Udbrud," *Skandinaven,* September 12, 1939.
26. *Skandinaven,* September 15, 1939.
27. *Skandinaven,* September 19, 1939.
28. *Skandinaven,* September 26, 1939.
29. "Det ulykkelige Polen," *Skandinaven,* October 6, 1939. Thaddeus Mitana, "Poland among the Powers," *Annals of the American Academy of Political and Social Science* 232, "A Challenge to Peacemakers" (March, 1944): 52–54.
30. "De nordiske Lande og Krigen," *Skandinaven,* October 6, 1939.
31. Lovoll, *Norwegian Newspapers,* 204.
32. "Amerikas Holdning," *Decorah-Posten,* September 12, 1939.
33. "Krigen skal holdes borte fra Amerika," *Decorah-Posten,* October 3, 1939.
34. "Breve fra Posten's Læsekreds," *Decorah-Posten,* October 6, 1939.
35. "Breve fra Posten's Læsekreds," *Decorah-Posten,* October 6, 1939.
36. "Bort fra Krigens Brændpunkt i Polen," *Decorah-Posten,* September 15, 1939.
37. Decorah-Posten, September 19, 1939.
38. One reader referred to Hitler as a better strategist than Mussolini in that the former did not provoke wars; instead, he only "liberated" people. Here, the reader refers to the annexation of Austria and the Sudetenland in Czechoslovakia by Nazi Germany in 1938. Rusk og Rask, *Decorah-Posten,* September 22, 1939.
39. Roald Lund's Column, *Washington Posten,* September 8, 1939.
40. "Polens Hovedstad Falt for Tolvte Gang Paa 700 Aar," *Washington Posten,* December 22, 1939.
41. "Impulsive Ord av Knut Hamsun," *Nordisk Tidende,* September 7, 1939.
42. Carl Søyland, "Om vi selger Livet vaart vil vi ha noe for det," *Nordisk Tidende,* September 14, 1939.
43. Tyskerne nær Warschau," *Decorah-Posten,* September 15; "Stor russisk hær rykker ind i Polen," *Decorah-Posten,* September 19; "Warschaus Overgivelse finder formelt Sted i dag," *Decorah-Posten,* September 29; and "Hitler vil tilby Fred nu," *Decorah-Posten,* October 3, 1939.
44. The Soviet Union demanded the lease of the Hanko Peninsula for thirty years in order to establish a naval base there. It demanded the cession of islands in the Gulf of Finland in southern Finland and the Rybachy Peninsula and the harbor near Petsamo in northern Finland. The Soviet Union also demanded that Finland move the border between Ladoga Lake and the Gulf of Finland 30 kilometers to the west and destroy Finnish fortifications on the Karelian Isthmus. Robert Edwards, *Hvit død. Russlands krig mot Finland 1939–40* (Oslo, 2007), 55, 65–69; Beevor, *Den andre verdenskrig,* 57–59.
45. Roald Lund, "The Finns Become Scandinavians," *Washington Posten,* October 20, 1939.
46. "Finland," *Skandinaven,* December 5, 1939.
47. "Finland og Kampen for Hjemlandet," *Skandinaven,* January 16, 1940.
48. Karen Dearlove, "From Europe to the Nation: American Journalistic Perceptions of

European International Relations, 1933–1941" (PhD diss., McMaster University, 2009), 241–44, 249. Dorothy Thompson, *New York Herald Tribune,* October 11, 1939.

49. "Finsk Modstand gjør det hedt for Russerne," *Skandinaven,* December 8, 1939.
50. "Et Folk i Nød," *Nordisk Tidende,* December 7, 1939.
51. Roald Lund, "Merket det stend . . . ," *Washington Posten,* December 8, 1939.
52. E. J. Vickner, "Finland, Vaart Broderfolk," *Washington Posten,* December 8, 1939.
53. Lund, "Merket."
54. Byron Nordstrom, *Scandinavia since 1500* (Minneapolis, 2000), 296–97.
55. "Norden mot Russland?," *Nordisk Tidende,* December 14, 1939.
56. The Finns had defeated the Russian 44th Division, which normally consisted of fifteen thousand troops, killed thousands of men, and taken more than a thousand prisoners. Reporters in various Norwegian-language newspapers in the United States stressed Russian losses and Finnish progress in the Winter War. "Finnernes Fremgang," *Fergus Falls Ukeblad,* January 10, 1940; "Soviet arme paa flukt," *Grand Forks Skandinav,* February 2, 1940; "Holder stand mot Russerne," *Grand Forks Skandinav,* February 16, 1940.
57. "Krigen," *Reform,* February 29, 1940; "Russerne rykker frem," *Grand Forks Skandinav,* March 1, 1940; "Russiske Seire," *Decorah-Posten,* March 1, 1940.
58. "Finland," *Decorah-Posten,* March 15, 1940.
59. "Finnland [sic] kjemper for hele Nordens sak," *Grand Forks Skandinav,* March 1, 1940.
60. Mark David Kuss, "Collective Security or World Domination: The Soviet Union and Germany, 1917–1939," (PhD diss., Louisiana State University, 2012), 118–19, 126–29, 139–41.
61. Roald Lund, "And Norway Finland's Battle," *Washington Posten,* January 26, 1940.
62. "Finlænderne holder Stand," *Skandinaven,* January 2, 1940.
63. "I den ellevte Time," *Nordisk Tidende,* January 18, 1940.
64. "Smilet dekker Norges Alvor mens Øiet vendes østover," *Nordisk Tidende,* February 8, 1940.
65. "Fremdeles finsk seir," *Skandinaven,* February 16, 1940.
66. "Finland Treger Hjelp," *Washington Posten,* March 8, 1940.
67. "Salute to the Brave" (originally by *New York Times*), *Nordisk Tidende,* February 22, 1940.
68. "Finlands Kamp," *Skandinaven,* February 20, 1940.
69. Paul W. Doerr, "'Frigid but Unprovocative': British Policy toward the USSR from the Nazi-Soviet Pact to the Winter War, 1939," *Journal of Contemporary History* 36: 3 (July, 2001): 438; James William Treu, "Search for an Ism: British Policy in the Russo-Finnish War of 1939–40" (PhD diss., University of Missouri-Kansas City, 2003), 291; Trygve Lie, *Hjemover* (Oslo, 1958), 121–31; Robert K. Garman, "Norway and the Bear: Soviet Coercive Diplomacy and Norwegian Security Policy," *International Security* 7:2 (Fall 1982): 56.
70. "Den rusiske-finske Krigstilstand er endt," *Skandinaven,* March 15, 1940.
71. Dr. E. J. Vickner, "Finland and Scandinavia," *Washington Posten,* March 22, 1940.
72. Jason Lavery, *The History of Finland* (Westport, Conn.: Greenwood Press, 2006), 120.
73. "Norge og Finland," *Nordisk Tidende,* March 21, 1940.
74. Lavery, *History of Finland,* 120.
75. "Breve fra Posten's Læsekreds," *Decorah-Posten,* February 16, 1940; "Sympatien for Finland faar Udslag I smaa og store Bidrag fra U.S.A.," *Reform,* February 29, 1940.

76. "Breve fra Posten's Læsekreds," *Decorah-Posten,* February 23, 1940.
77. "De Døde i Sneen," *Nordisk Tidende,* January 4, 1940.
78. "Hjelp til Finland er indirekte hjelp til det norske folk," *Fergus Falls Ukeblad,* January 24, 1940.
79. "Kom og hjælp!," *Decorah-Posten,* March 8, 1940.
80. In September of 1939 Herbert Hoover had launched the idea that neutral north European countries could establish an international committee to "watch and report" conditions regarding "examples of war operations toward the civilian population." Its mission was to find out whether war had affected women and children deliberately, and according to Hoover the commission could be organized by Sweden, Norway, Denmark, Finland, Holland, and Belgium. He put forward the idea that this committee would be accepted by countries that were at war and by all other neutral countries. "Mod Grusomhed," *Decorah-Posten,* September 19, 1939.
81. Finnish credit for purchase of goods in the United States would be given to the Finnish-American Trading Corporation, an American corporation organized by the Finnish minister with a paid capital of $1 million. The loan was to be guaranteed by the Bank of Finland or the government of Finland. "Hjælp til Finland," *Decorah-Posten,* December 12, 1939.
82. Members were Frederick R. Bay, Dr. Aasgaard (Bishop, Pres Norw Luth Church in America), Arthur Andersen (styret i NAHA), E. B. Hauke (Pres Sons of Norway International), Olaf Halvorsen (in Los Angeles), S. J. Arnesen (Major, Brooklyn, N.Y.). *Reform,* March 31, 1940.
83. Frederick R. Bay was chairman of the Norwegian division of the national Finnish Relief Fund, Inc. *Reform,* January 25, 1940.
84. All told, the committee collected $18,593,78 for the relief work. "Minneapolis og St. Paul," *Decorah-Posten,* January 12, 1940.
85. The Sons of Norway was a fraternal organization founded in 1895 in Minneapolis for the purpose of protecting members and their families from the financial hardships experienced during times of sickness and death in the family, Sons of Norway: History [cited May 2, 2019]. Online: https: //www.sofn.com/about_us/history/.
86. "Hjelp til det ulykkelige finske folk," *Fergus Falls Ukeblad,* December 27, 1939.
87. "Hjelp til det ulykkelige finske folk," *Fergus Falls Ukeblad,* December 27, 1939.
88. For example, on February 6, 1940, the *Decorah-Posten* announced that Heimbygda Lodge of Sons of Norway in Lanesboro, Minnesota, had contributed a total of $150 for the Finnish Relief Fund. There were also significant contributions from individuals in Lanesboro and vicinity. Around the same time the press noted that the Fridtjof Lodge in Petersburg, N. D., had collected $105 for the relief fund. "Decorah og Omegn," *Decorah-Posten,* February 6, 1940; "Finnenes hjelpefond," *Grand Forks Skandinav,* January 26, 1940.
89. "Skisteævner i U.S.A. til Indtægt for det finske Hjælpefond," *Reform*, February 1, 1940; "Bidragene til det finske Hjælpefond kommer fra hele U.S.," *Reform,* February 15, 1940; Sympatien for Finland faar Udslag i smaa og store Bidrag fra U.S.A.," *Reform,* February 29, 1940.
90. In late January of 1940, Minnesota governor Harold E. Stassen was the main speaker at a large rally for Meeker and Wright Counties, Minnesota, at Cokato. The main purpose of the event was to begin collecting funds for the suffering Finns. Around fifteen hundred people participated in the rally. "Nyheder fra Nordveststaterne, Minnesota," *Decorah-Posten,* February 2, 1940.

91. A regular collection campaign in Decorah proved very successful, and by March 6 a total of $1,155,38 had been collected for the Finnish Relief Fund. "Decorah og Omegn," *Decorah-Posten,* March 8, 1940.
92. Newspapers announced that individuals could purchase maps of Finland in color and a brief history of the country from the Norwegian-American division of the Finnish Relief Fund. See for example "Kart over Finland," *Decorah-Posten,* March 19, 1940.
93. This was a national organization which aimed at collecting money for purchasing airplanes, rifles, and ammunition for the Finnish army. The national organization in the United States was divided in subcommittees based on ethnic background, including a Danish-American, a Norwegian-American, and a Swedish-American committee. "Prominente Skandinaver slutter sig til Organisasjonen Fighting-Funds for Finnland [sic]," *Visergutten,* March 7, 1940.
94. "Efter Freden," *Skandinaven,* March 22, 1940.
95. Roald Lund, "The War Is Not Over Yet!," *Washington Posten,* March 29, 1940.
96. "Finsk-russisk Krig endt," *Decorah-Posten,* March 15, 1940.
97. "Finlandshjælpen," *Decorah-Posten,* March 22, 1940; *Reform,* March 31, 1940.
98. "Breve fra Posten's Læsekreds," *Decorah-Posten,* April 12, 1940. We may add that in addition to the relief fund, the U.S. Congress offered a $20 million loan to Finland in early March of 1940. The House Banking Committee suggested that Export-Import Bank's capital be increased by $100 million. Federal loan administrator Jesse Jones had talks with the committee to loan $20 million to Finland in addition to $10 million already received. Sweden and Norway would also be given $10 million each for purchases in the United States. The U.S. loan was also extended to countries in South America. On March 6 a majority in the House of Representatives voted in favor, with the result that up to $20 million of a total of $100 million could be given to one single country for the purchase of non-military goods. The loan did not serve its purpose, however, as the war ended soon after. "Laanet til Finland," *Fergus Falls Ukeblad,* February 28, 1940; "Finland faar Laan," *Fergus Falls Ukeblad,* March 6, 1940; "Finland faar Laan," *Decorah-Posten,* March 1, 1940.
99. Roald Lund, "Fattening Finland for Slaughter," *Washington Posten,* February 16, 1940.
100. Roald Lund, "Finns Become Scandinavians."
101. Karen Dearlove, "From Europe to the Nation," 237–41.
102. Joranger, "Lokale eller nasjonale kollektive identiteter?," 232–37.

Campaigns on the Home Front

NORWEGIAN-AMERICAN FARMERS AND WORKERS MOBILIZED FOR WAR

Ann Marie Legreid

"But there is one front and one battle where everyone in the United States, every man, woman, and child . . . is in action. That front is right here at home."[1]

—PRESIDENT FRANKLIN D. ROOSEVELT, 1942

Norwegians and Norwegian Americans were united as never before by the ideals of liberty in the wake of the Nazi invasion of Norway on April 9, 1940. The free world and its basic human freedoms were at stake. The citizens of Stoughton, Wisconsin, were "outraged" at the "ruthless invasion of Norway" which had "all the earmarks of piracy."[2] Sunday, April 21, 1940, was declared a day of prayer for the people of Norway and their royal family by Norwegian Lutheran congregations across America. Norwegian Americans incorporated American Relief for Norway within ten days of the Nazi invasion. The Nazi occupation (1940–1945) generated both sympathy and support for the Norwegian people among Norwegian Americans. Norwegian Americans were intimately and passionately involved in wartime efforts on the home front and on the frontlines, revealing strong and enduring ties to a beloved motherland. From confusion and despair, a united and determined people emerged with the common cause of liberty.

King Haakon, speaking to the Norwegian people in 1940 via radio from Northern Norway on the Norwegian national holiday, the Seventeenth of May, said: "For more than a hundred years this day has united the people of Norway in the idea of liberty and the work of liberty accomplished at Eidsvold, where we all promised one another to defend this country." The King's monogram H7 became the symbol of liberty. C. J. Hambro, president of the Norwegian parliament, wrote in the wake of the invasion: "And so the Government urges the whole nation to safeguard the inheritance of freedom, faithful to the great ideas which have carried Norway through the centuries. Long live the fatherland! Long live a free Norway!"[3]

In 1940 Norwegians in America were heavily concentrated in urban areas and farming communities in the Upper Midwest. Minneapolis and Chicago were the undisputed centers for Norwegian-American organizational life. The earliest settlements were planted in northern Illinois and southern Wisconsin in the mid-nineteenth century. Eventually, colonies emerged across the United States and Canada, in Minnesota, Iowa, Nebraska, Kansas, Michigan, the Dakotas, the Canadian prairies, Texas, Washington, California, Vancouver, and New York. The great transatlantic migrations brought more than 900,000 Norwegians to the United States from 1825 to the present day, with 87 percent of them migrating between 1865 and 1930. Thus, connections to the motherland were vibrant and meaningful when war came to Norway in 1940.[4]

Wartime stresses and strains brought solidarity to Norwegian Americans from all walks of life, heightened their patriotic spirit as Americans, and provided new opportunities for them in areas such as business, industry, and agricultural production. Home-front campaigns were organized across America by innumerable ethnic, charitable, and community groups. Norwegian Americans, like their ethnic neighbors, joined the home-front campaigns in very personal and generous ways.

Norwegian Americans served alongside their fellow Americans on the battlefield as well. In doing so, they brought heightened visibility in the United States to the plight of the people in occupied Norway.[5] In September 1942 President Roosevelt noted the resilience and resistance of the Norwegian people in his famous words to the free world delivered in Washington, D.C., from his open car, with Princess Märtha at his side, "Look to Norway!"[6] Roosevelt's Four Freedoms speech posited moral obligations that transcended national and ethnic boundaries: freedom from fear, freedom from want, freedom of speech, and freedom of worship. The Four Freedoms were the subject of iconic paintings by Norman Rockwell replicated on calendars and posters and displayed ubiquitously in homes and public places across America. Throughout the war these hung as important visual reminders of the basic freedoms at stake.[7]

Americans engaged in the war effort fought for the universal values of life, liberty, and the pursuit of happiness, the ideals of a liberal democracy. They also felt private moral obligations to family, the nonpolitical obligation of a father defending his family from fascist aggression. The American moral imagination was replete with images and concepts of protecting loved ones against the aggressor nation. Husbands and fathers, in particular, acted on a moral obligation to protect the unprotected, their families.[8] The famous Hollywood pinups of Rita Hayworth, Betty Grable, and Jane Russell were reminders of wives, mothers, and sweethearts, and the moral obligation of the protector to protect loved ones at home. Soldiers decorated their war machines with images of the Grables, Hayworths, and soldier girlfriends. These "painted icons of femininity" were "good-luck talismans," representing the women and the homes for whom they were fighting. Norwegian Americans, too, were fighting for home and family and the ideals of liberal democracy.[9]

When the Norwegian relief agency was founded in Chicago in April 1940, its founders resolved "that we, at all times, diligently shall demonstrate our faith in an Ultimate Justice, that the people of our old Motherland shall not for long be subjected to a rule that destroys a social order founded on freedom and intelligence." There was a similar resolution by the Norwegian Lutheran Church in America and a commitment of $100,000 in order "that the National Lutheran Council might launch immediately a program of wartime services." The National Lutheran Council, binding Lutherans since 1918, nearly extinct in the thirties, "suddenly assumed new life in the face of the wartime emergencies."[10] The war ushered in an era of unprecedented unity and cooperation between Lutheran groups in support of war relief, war orphans, and other war-related matters of common concern.

American Relief for Norway worked closely with Lutheran groups to promote "a large-scale nationwide relief effort among people of Norwegian birth and ancestry—from New York to San Francisco."[11] In just over a year, American Relief for Norway collected over $520,000.[12] Local congregations like those in Trempealeau County, Wisconsin were determined to follow the lead and support the war effort. They sponsored special fundraisers, clothing drives, and special ceremonies for war relief and to honor those who served. On April 21, 1940, congregants at North Beaver Creek Lutheran, led in the Norwegian language by Pastor Sweger, joined in prayer and singing of the Norwegian national anthem. Pastor Urberg of the neighboring congregation wrote: "The Norwegian relief organization will soon be in action. Many will wish to take part in this relief work of blood relatives and the Norwegian pastors will be glad to help you get your gifts to their destination of love and mercy."[13]

The Norwegian Lutheran congregation in Hawkins, Wisconsin, sponsored a church festival for the Seventeenth of May in 1941. Waldemar Ager, journalist from Eau Claire, Wisconsin, spoke and the guests were served ethnic treats of lefse, graut, and Norwegian baking. They collected $60 for Norwegian relief at this event, this sum in addition to numerous drives and donations throughout the year, all aid to Norway.[14] Immanuel Lutheran Congregation in Benson, Minnesota held a Seventeenth of May service in 1942 in the Norwegian language. The congregational choir sang the Norwegian and American national anthems. The Sons of Norway Bjorgvin Lodge in Benson sponsored a "Syttende Mai" Benefit Ball in May of 1942, a fundraiser for American Relief for Norway.[15] Church-sponsored fundraising was a key element in the work of the relief agency.

The Second World War was a total war in the sense that it mobilized the American population and utilized America's new mass culture in myriad and innovative ways, especially in war propaganda. Much of that war propaganda, unlike in previous wars, came from private initiatives and the popular press. In the Upper Midwest, Norwegian-American farm families were informed of the Nazi invasion and the progress of the war in a variety of formats, including radio broadcasts with war news, many reports from London, and Roosevelt's famous fireside chats. People read local newspapers such as the *La Crosse Tribune* and *Stoughton Courier Hub,* which featured stories about local soldiers and updates provided by the U.S. War Department. They read farm journals such as the *Wisconsin Agriculturalist,* which gave much attention to food production and providing hardware for the war effort. Those who could read Norwegian poured over *Decorah-Posten,* often passed hand to hand, home to home, certainly with some translations, each one including poignant reminders of wartime clashes and casualties.

The phrase "they also served," was commonly used to identify and applaud the men and women who worked in home-front farming and industry. The U.S. Department of Agriculture created the federal Crop Corps to nurture and assure the nation's food supply, and the Corps, in turn, oversaw the work of the Women's Land Army and Victory Farm Volunteers. American farmers and farm laborers were classified as "war personnel" and excused from official service in the U.S. military. Volunteerism, victory gardens, rationing, and salvage campaigns were among the many strategies that engaged Norwegian Americans, rural and urban, in building Roosevelt's massive "arsenal for democracy."[16]

The U.S. War Department issued war propaganda of assorted varieties, much of it aimed at building and sustaining the war industries, and that included many aspects of agricultural production. Drawing on material from the War Department, the *Wisconsin Agriculturalist* was loaded with articles, visuals, and ads that implored its readers to join the war effort: "Harvest the Crops of Freedom," and "Your Barn Is a Victory Plant for More Milk," "Patriot Gardens Painted in Color," and "Help Keep Their Guns Loaded."[17] County Defense Boards (later War Boards) were established in communities across America with the charge to coordinate local war efforts and to increase agricultural production. Representatives from various federal agencies were assigned to the county level to coordinate and direct war-related initiatives. Guaranteed prices were put on critical foods as, for example, eggs at twenty-two cents per dozen, part of the "eggs for defense" campaign.

With the attack on Pearl Harbor in December 1941 came orders to ration strategic items like gasoline and farm machinery, efforts overseen by local rationing boards. In Renville County, Minnesota, volunteer women were designated Victory Aids and charged with collecting books for soldiers and soliciting contributions to the Red Cross, USO, American Relief for Norway, and other war-effort entities.

The U.S. War Department promoted the planting of victory gardens as a means of increasing the food supply at home and abroad, thus supplementing school lunch programs and providing much-needed seed for the next growing season. Seed exports were arranged for war-torn Europe. The County Extension Office in Renville County appointed Neighborhood Leaders; these teams coordinated meetings and demonstrations on topics such as home canning, vegetable storage, maintenance of farm machinery, and the construction of homemade labor-saving devices like hay stackers and range feeders. For the farm wife, there was instruction on resource-saving methods like recipes with sugar substitutes and sewing

Figure 1. Girl Scouts examine a portion of a victory garden in San Francisco, ca. 1943. Photograph by Ann Roesner. Courtesy of the Library of Congress, Prints & Photographs Division, Farm Security Administration/Office of War Information Black-and-White Negatives.

Figure 2. Professor Harry Nelson teaches his daughter and her fellow Girl Scouts the basics of gardening in a victory garden, ca. 1943. Photograph by Ann Roesner. Courtesy of the Library of Congress, Prints & Photographs Division, Farm Security Administration/Office of War Information Black-and-White Negatives.

tips for conserving fabric, such as shorter skirts and smaller lapels. In 1942 the Farm Bureau Women of Caledonia, Minnesota, organized a special presentation titled, "Feeding the Family for Health, Morale, and Victory."[18]

County labor committees oversaw employment centers, recruited farm workers, and placed them on farms by need. Henry Torbenson, County Labor Director in Renville County, recruited part-time farm workers from nearby villages, especially high school youth, who proved to be valuable through the growing seasons. He had less success with the urban youth from Minneapolis. The federal government allowed the hiring of foreign labor (1942–1947) which resulted in a considerable migration of Mexican braceros into the northern states. Among Norwegian-American farmers, the braceros were utilized mainly for the grain harvest and corn picking, as were German POWs on some occasions. However, Norwegian-American farmers made little use of the Women's Land Army, sometimes called "farmerettes" or "tractorettes," a federal program that recruited women from the cities to do farm labor. Norwegian-American farmers preferred to use their own wives and daughters for farm projects and harvests.[19]

Wisconsin, like other agricultural states, recorded unprecedented growth in its crop acreage and animal industries during the war, particularly in the areas of milk, meat, eggs, and vegetable production. Farm production grew markedly in response to favorable weather and wartime demand. Increases were recorded in family incomes, land values, farm wages, and acreage devoted to feed crops (corn and oats) and new crops like soybeans and hemp. Hemp was an important wartime material for cords, ropes, and parachutes. Commodity prices doubled and gross farm income increased 160 percent during the war years. Farms were labeled "arsenals of food" and farmers were the volunteer "land army."[20] This production was quite remarkable given the severe shortages attributed to the war, especially in farm labor, gasoline and oil, parts for machinery, fertilizer, and animal feed.[21]

The Second World War had a lasting impact on Norwegian-American farmers and farmworkers, farm and household production, and farming methods. Higher farm incomes meant more money for war bonds, farm improvement, and aid campaigns for war-torn Europe, including American Relief for Norway. In addition to collecting financial donations, American Relief for Norway also organized and coordinated clothing and shoe drives and exports of dried milk, meats, and vegetables, sent to Norway under the auspices of Sweden's Red Cross or through occupied Denmark. The war also generated great geographical mobility as farmers and farm laborers took jobs in the war industries, creating labor shortages on the farm and prompting the consolidation of two or more farms under single management. This, in turn, encouraged more retired farmers to stay on farms and to cultivate more gardens. For women, both urban and rural, the war brought new opportunities and expectations and liberation from traditional roles as house- and farmwives. Women turned rivets in industries and occupied managerial and leadership positions in business, industry, agriculture, and public service.[22]

Civilian defense teams led campaigns for the sale of war bonds as well as scrap drives to collect metal and other resources needed for the war. These campaigns often developed into full-blown competitions between schools, service clubs, towns, and counties. Carmen Moe of Coon Valley, Wisconsin remembers

Figure 3. Wisconsin farm junk drive, Waupaca, Wisconsin, 1942. McCormick-International Harvester Collection (6560). Courtesy of the Wisconsin Historical Society.

the campaign to collect milkweed floss, bags of it to be processed and used as insulation for special combat equipment.[23] "Rationing of gasoline, rubber, and sugar went into effect," she wrote, and "coupon books were issued to individuals and to families. Nylons became scarce—nylon was needed for the manufacture of parachutes for soldiers and pilots. We saved the flattened tin cans as there was a shortage of aluminum for the construction of airplanes. Other metals were in short supply. Carin Halla personally smashed all of her Swedish copperware and gave it to the metal drive in Madison—Carin hated the Nazis."[24] Olaf Larson, a young lad in Edgerton, Wisconsin, recalled collecting walnut shells by the bagful; they were used in the production of wartime gas masks. Farmers were encouraged by ads in agricultural papers to collect old tires and discarded machinery for scrap drives. State salvage committees sponsored drives to collect rubber, tin cans, cooking fats for explosives, newspapers, and silk stockings for parachutes. Norwegian farmers in southwest Wisconsin began harvesting basswood for sale to the government; being lightweight, it was ideal for airplane and lifeboat construction.[25] One Norwegian-American farmer recalled the government freeze on new machinery, being told that he had to take a tractor off the lot by midnight if he wanted one; after midnight, sales would be frozen. He drove his first tractor home in the middle of the night.[26]

The Council of Bygdelags in America (bygdelag were regional associations based on Norwegian roots), issued a statement of solidarity with the Norwegian people following the German attack, but with the war came major and unanticipated changes to the bygdelag. The attack on Pearl Harbor and entry of the United States into the war riveted national attention on the war effort. Bygdelag meetings were not held in 1942, and fewer "stevner" (conventions) were held in the interests of redirecting resources to win the war.[27]

The Red Cross and Sons and Daughters of Norway in La Crosse collected money and donations for American Relief for Norway in a multitude of ways. The *La Crosse Tribune* reported in November 1941, "After clothing and shoes have been collected and repaired they will be cleaned, moth-proofed and boxed for one of the four or five Norwegian governmental warehouses throughout the United States."[28] Red Cross ships transported the goods through the war zone to the Swedish Red Cross for eventual distribution.[29] Support also reached Camp Little Norway in Toronto, Canada, and Norwegian seamen exiled in London.[30] There were strict procedures and blockades intended to protect deliveries, yet sometimes the deliveries fell into the hands of the German occupiers and did not reach their intended destinations. Food and clothing were smuggled into Norway by an organized underground working with the Norwegian Church in Sweden, a dangerous operation, but one that supplied much-needed food and goods to parishes throughout Norway.[31]

James Axel Trane emigrated with his parents from Målselven, Troms og Finnmark county, to rural Wisconsin in 1864. Not content to turn the soil, James left the family farm and moved to the nearest sizable city, La Crosse, where he gained employment with the W. A. Roosevelt Company, learned plumbing engineering, and subsequently founded his own plumbing firm. With his son, Reuben,

Figure 4. Women knitting socks to send to Norway during the German occupation. American Relief for Norway, Inc., papers, 1940–1946 (P646). Courtesy of the Norwegian-American Historical Association, Northfield, Minnesota.

Figure 5. Map indicating the location of efforts to send clothing and other items to Norwegians during occupation. American Relief for Norway, Inc. papers, 1940–1946 (P646). Courtesy of the Norwegian-American Historical Association, Northfield, Minnesota.

he built a heating and plumbing business that took on large government contracts during the two world wars. For the Second World War, the Trane firm developed heating, cooling, and ventilating systems for warships, airplanes, and military plants. Together they pioneered the first all-aluminum aircraft radiator and equipment to prevent ice formation on airplane wings. The Trane Company employed hundreds of Norwegian Americans eager to support the war by industrial production on the home front.[32]

The Norwegian-American press was profoundly important in fundraising for the war effort. The pages of *Decorah-Posten* overflowed with war news throughout the occupation, including such pieces as passionate speeches by King Haakon and Crown Prince Olav, patriotic songs and poems, editorials deploring the Nasjonal Samling (Nazi party), updates on Norwegian war dead, and state-by-state reporting on donations to Norwegian relief known as "Norgeshjelpen." The newspaper was replete with stories and information for giving to the war effort, dollars as well as material goods. The intensity and passion of the war reporting was notable. The paper ran a column, Hjemmefronten, reporting on "home-front" responses to the occupation, such as student demonstrations in Oslo against Quisling, sabotage in Stavanger, Nazi roundups and executions, and the singing of "*Ja vi elsker*" (Yes, we love Norway) in Copenhagen at the seventieth birthday celebration for King Christian. Headlines such as, "The New Order in Norway," "Norway under the Iron Heel," and "A Fundamental Break with the Constitution" were gut-wrenching and common. In all of this, there was one resounding and overarching theme in the printed media: "*Norge vil bli et frit land igjen!*" (Norway will be a free country again).[33]

Decorah-Posten also advertised books on the war effort for sale, none more widely read and impactful in Nordic America than C. J. Hambro's *I Saw It Happen in Norway,* published by Decorah's Anundsen Press (1940). Hambro recounts eyewitness details of the invasion and the circuitous maneuvers that took the royal family and government to relative safety. Published in English, it was no doubt intended to reach a large audience with a desperate call to action for what was at stake: life and liberty. In November 1940 Hambro was in Decorah to speak on the war effort, part of a speaking circuit that took him to urban and rural communities across the country. *Decorah-Posten* reported that Norwegians turned out in large numbers to get every morsel of Norway news. Carmen Moe, in Coon Valley, remembers her grandfather reading to her about war-torn Norway from *Decorah-Posten*. She also recalled the long military convoys on the highway between La Crosse and the army's Camp McCoy. She wrote later in life, "There was a widespread feeling of disbelief and aversion for Hitler and the calamitous events taking place in Europe."[34]

Letters from family in Norway were printed regularly in *Decorah-Posten*. Inga Fredrikstad, Brandbu, Norway, wrote to her sister in Edmond, Washington, "*Vi lever i en urolig tid*" (We live in a troubled time). She noted rising prices and food shortages, with food taken from Norwegian farms for export to Germany. Inga indicated that she would like to write more, but could not, since letters were opened and censored.[35] The same month *Decorah-Posten* reported that Crown Prince Olav was visiting America, and published an editorial titled "Norway and Eidsvold."[36] That was followed in the next issue by Roosevelt's words, "America . . . an arsenal for democracy." Through the war era there were ongoing references to Lincoln's Gettysburg Address in the American media. *Decorah-Posten* reported that school children across Norway were memorizing the address; they could not recite it aloud for fear of Nazi punishment, but they recited it quietly and in private with sure conviction.[37] On the Seventeenth of May, 1940, the *Stoughton Courier Hub* published the famous quote in Norwegian: "*et en regjering av folket, ved folket, og for folket aldrig skal forsvinde fra jorden*" (that government of the people, by the people, for the people shall not perish from the earth).

The juxtaposition of items in *Decorah-Posten* was often quite odd and ironic, for example a photo of Heinrich Himmler next to the local Livestock and Grain report. It published the St. Olaf college radio schedule, which included segments such as Hymns We Love alongside The Farm Report, For National Defense, and Norway and the War with guest Einar Lund. There were heart-wrenching articles titled "Norwegians in Concentration Camps," and abundant patriotic expressions for each Seventeenth of May, knowing it could not be celebrated in Norway.[38] *Decorah-Posten* reported that Crown Prince Olav's radio broadcast to the Norwegian people from London, "*har gjort stort virkning*" (has made a big impact) on them.[39] On October 22, 1940, a radiogram from Helsingfors to *Decorah-Posten* announced that the last two ships would soon sail from Petsamo to North America, thereafter that route would be closed. Sigrid Undset, unable to travel by steamship from Sweden, fled the Nazis through Russia and Japan in an arduous journey that finally landed her in Brooklyn, a refugee who wrote in heartfelt terms: "Help from our kinsfolk in America will come as a blessing and will be received with fervent gratitude."[40] Many prominent Norwegian Americans, including linguist Einar Haugen, wrote and lectured on the war effort in Norwegian America, engagements that were widely known and publicized in *Decorah-Posten.*

Words and maps focused on the "Faedreland" or fatherland, and occasional anti-Hitler cartoons and editorials lauded the efforts of resistance fighters in Norway. Dr. Kathleen Stokker's pioneering work, *Folklore Fights the Nazis,* utilizes wartime joke books and diaries, interviews, and testimonials to show the importance of folk life and humor in Norway's resistance movement.[41] Belittling Hitler, anti-Nazi sentiments, impudence, and confrontation were common themes in Norwegian America just as they were in occupied Norway. Norwegian-American artists provided striking poster and calendar art for the war campaigns. For example, Carl Holte of Duluth, Minnesota, created a poster showing the Norwegian flag in red, white, blue, and black, the lower half black in smoldering ruins and a Norwegian girl extending her arms upward. The caption: "Norwegian Relief—Help Norway."[42]

After five long years, Norway was finally liberated; church bells rang, people danced, and Norwegian flags were hoisted. The Norwegian-American press shifted its themes to celebration, American prosperity, and rebuilding war-ravaged Norway. In Wisconsin, Pastor Konrad Urberg announced plans for a V-Day observance in the three Urberg congregations. One hour after the official announcement that war hostilities had ceased, worship services would be held at his congregation in Blair, three hours after the announcement in Ettrick, and five hours after the announcement in North Beaver Creek.[43] The rejoicing reverberated across the ocean.

Congregations and secular organizations of Norwegian heritage engaged in war-relief efforts with vigor, much of it coordinated by state committees and funneled through American Relief for Norway. No less than 156 million kroner in money and goods was delivered to Norway during and following the war. Thirteen thousand garments had been knitted by various knitting and women's clubs through the war years; ninety thousand Christmas packages and 1.5 million chocolate bars had been delivered. Anfin Sather of North Dakota, born in Sogn, established a trust fund under the auspices of American Relief for Norway to support the organization of Norwegian agricultural clubs.[44] These efforts were the tip of the iceberg in wartime and postwar relief.

In April 1946 Eleanor Roosevelt published an article in *Ladies' Home Journal* imploring the public to send care packages to war-ravaged countries, including Norway. The response helped hundreds of families across Norway through donations of food, clothing, and other useful items.[45] Between April 1948 and December 1951, the Marshall Plan infused more than $13 billion into seventeen war-ravaged countries in western and southern Europe. Marshall funding helped to rehabilitate Norway's economy and structure a new Europe with open markets and free trade.

Rural or urban, people were united in home-front campaigns for liberty, Christian ideals, and basic moralism. Ethnic heritage and motherland were deeply meaningful to Norwegians in America. They were also patriotic Americans interested in seeing a democratic, sovereign Norway emerge. For as much as they wanted to focus on their peaceful lives in rural America, on their crops and cattle, Norwegian Americans were swept into the broader international currents, the fight for humanity, the fight for those four basic freedoms. They rose to the occasion in innovative and resolute ways, working with fellow Americans, making sacrifices in very personal and generous ways. Publications like the *Wisconsin Agriculturalist* and *Decorah-Posten* were instrumental in informing and engaging Norwegian-American farmers in war relief and war-related industries. When the war ended, Norwegians in America were united in pride and celebration with all Americans. President Lincoln's famous words had prevailed: "*et en regjering av folket, ved folket, og for folket aldrig skal forsvinde fra jorden*" (that government of the people, by the people, and for the people shall not perish from the earth). "*Norge vil bli et frit land igjen*" (Norway will be a free country again).

Ann Marie Legreid *is Professor of Geography at Shepherd University in Shepherdstown, West Virginia, a public liberal arts institution. She earned her PhD and MS in Historical Geography from the University of Wisconsin–Madison. Her specialties are European and North American geography, cultural geography, population and development, and migration studies.*

NOTES

1. "On Our National Economic Policy: Radio Address of the President on the Subject of Total War and Total Effort," delivered April 28, 1942, Washington, D.C.
2. *Stoughton Courier Hub,* April 10, 1940.
3. King Haakon and Hambro are quoted extensively in C. J. Hambro, *I Saw It Happen In Norway* (Decorah, Iowa, 1940).
4. Odd S. Lovoll, "Norwegian Americans," [cited April 14, 2020]. Online: https://www.everyculture.com/multi/Le-Pa/Norwegian-Americans.html. In the present day, Minnesota leads in the number of citizens of Norwegian ancestry, followed by Wisconsin, California, Washington, and North Dakota.
5. Odd S. Lovoll, *Norwegians on the Prairie: Ethnicity and the Development of the Country Town* (St. Paul, 2006), 249.
6. A. N. Rygg, *American Relief for Norway* (Brooklyn, N.Y., 1947), 34. American Relief for Norway was led by representatives from numerous Norwegian-American groups, including the Norwegian Lutheran Church of America, Daughters of Norway, Women's Missionary Federation, and Sons of Norway.
7. Robert B. Westbrook, *Why We Fought: Forging American Obligations in World War II* (Washington, D.C., 2010), 44–48. The four freedoms are articulated in Roosevelt's Fireside Chat 20: "On the Progress of the War," delivered February 23, 1942.
8. Westbrook, *Why We Fought,* 31.
9. Westbrook, *Why We Fought,* 39–65.
10. E. Clifford Nelson, *The Lutheran Church among Norwegian Americans,* vol. 2 (Minneapolis, 1960), 312.
11. Lovoll, *Norwegians on the Prairie,* 251.
12. Rygg, *American Relief for Norway,* 18.
13. Ann Marie Legreid, *One in the Spirit,* congregational history of the North Beaver Creek Lutheran Church, Trempealeau County, Wisconsin, 1984, 31.
14. Rygg, *American Relief for Norway,* 223–24.
15. Lovoll, *Norwegians on the Prairie,* 251.
16. Douglas Hurt, *The Great Plains during World War II* (Lincoln, Neb., 2008), 81–99; and for the industrial mobilization, see Maury Klein, *A Call to Arms: Mobilizing America for World War II* (New York, 2013), 511–35.
17. *Wisconsin Agriculturalist,* April 4, 1940; January 10, 1942; May 16, 1942; May 20, 1942.
18. *La Crosse Tribune,* La Crosse, Wisconsin, February 13, 1942, 6.
19. Doris Weatherford, *American Women and World War II* (Edison, N.J., 2009), 208–36;

and Stephanie Carpenter, *On the Home Front: The Women's Land Army in World War II* (DeKalb, Ill., 2003), 120–34.

20. *La Crosse Tribune,* February 13, 1942, 4.
21. Walter H. Ebling, Wisconsin State Department of Agriculture Bulletin, No. 243: 1–27.
22. Doris Weatherford, *American Women and World War II,* 191–93; Maury Klein, *A Call to Arms,* 520–25.
23. Carmen J. Moen, *Sleeps Not the Valley* (Minneapolis, 1999), 386.
24. Moen, *Sleeps Not the Valley,* 362.
25. *La Crosse Tribune,* February 3, 1942, 11.
26. Memoirs of Samuel O. Legreid, manuscript in the library of Ann Marie Legreid.
27. Odd S. Lovoll, *A Folk Epic: The Bygdelag in America* (Boston: Twayne Publishers, published for the Norwegian-American Historical Association, 1975), 195.
28. *La Crosse Tribune,* November 5, 1941, 8.
29. *La Crosse Tribune,* April 17, 1940, 2.
30. Ingrid Semmingsen, *Norway to America: A History of the Migration* (Minneapolis, 1978), 165.
31. Rygg, *American Relief for Norway,* 25–26.
32. *La Crosse Tribune,* September 7, 1954, 2. The Trane Company blossomed as the result of a brilliant combination of perseverance, entrepreneurial spirit, business finesse, and engineering know-how and innovation. Still rooted in La Crosse, Trane stands tall as a global giant in heating and cooling technologies to the present day.
33. For examples, see *Decorah-Posten,* November 1, 1940.
34. Moen, *Sleeps Not the Valley,* 385.
35. *Decorah-Posten,* June 25, 1940.
36. *Decorah-Posten,* December 27, 1940.
37. *Decorah-Posten,* October 29, 1940.
38. *Decorah-Posten,* December 3, 1940.
39. *Decorah-Posten,* October 15, 1940.
40. Rygg, *American Relief for Norway,* 95.
41. Kathleen Stokker, *Folklore Fights the Nazis: Humor in Occupied Norway, 1940–1945* (Madison, Wisc., 1995).
42. Rygg, *American Relief for Norway,* 95.
43. Legreid, *One in the Spirit,* 31.
44. Rygg, *American Relief for Norway,* 148–49.
45. Rygg, *American Relief for Norway,* 69.

Our Values Are in Danger

NORWEGIAN-AMERICAN RESPONSES TO WORLD WAR II IN THE PACIFIC NORTHWEST

Hans-Petter Grav

April 10, 1940, appeared to be like any other day in Portland. The downtown district west of the Willamette River bustled as it usually did on a weekday. People went about their business as always, browsing shops, muttering complaints about the spring weather, purposefully hurrying up and down the sidewalk on errands or on their way to reunite with waiting spouses. If anything had seemed unusual that day, it must have been the somber expressions on the faces of the sixty-two delegates for the Daughters of Norway of the Pacific Coast's Twenty-Second Biennial Convention as they arrived at the art deco Congress Hotel on Sixth and Main. Later that evening, the delegates wore attractive gowns and shared solemn looks as if attending a funeral as they made their way to the opening reception across the river in Norse Hall. Neither the members of the Sons of Norway Grieg Lodge, the hosts for the occasion, nor the Daughters of Norway delegates could possibly have known that the receptions, dinners, and meetings they had planned for weeks and months would so completely be dominated by the unimaginable news that Germany had made Norway a battleground the day prior.[1]

"We gave speeches, sang, and prayed for our motherland Norway," Inga Frodesen, the departing president, wrote of the convention. Organizers and delegates often interrupted the program, which included heartfelt and sympathetic speeches from both the governor of Oregon and the mayor of Portland, with "Song for Mother Norway," which left few dry eyes and brought attendees' thoughts to yesterday's headlines, though undoubtedly they needed little reminding.[2] As part of the order of business on the first convention day, they named Crown Princess Märtha of Norway an honorary member; wholeheartedly agreed with an appeal made by *Washington Posten,* a Norwegian-language weekly published in Seattle, to adopt the oath of the 1814 Constitutional Assembly; opened a relief fund; and committed all the member lodges "to do everything in their power to help their people in need."[3]

Norwegian Americans faced crisis in April 1940 as individuals and as a community. Perceived demands of assimilation and American loyalty represented a challenge to ethnic cultural retention during World War II as it had amid the nativist pressures of World War I. Despite the demands for loyalty during a time of war and the ethnic acculturation of the second, third, and fourth generations of Norwegian Americans, the Norwegian-American community in the Pacific Northwest proved remarkably cohesive throughout World War II. In the context of a homeland occupied by Nazi Germany, Pacific Northwest Norwegians felt a heightened responsibility to maintain, even enshrine, the collective memory and ethnic heritage of pre-Nazified Norway. The shock of the German occupation of Norway therefore undoubtedly boosted Norwegian identities among Pacific Northwest Norwegians, particularly prior to Pearl Harbor. More importantly, the World War II era sheds light on how a vibrant and healthy immigrant community, whose ethnic institutions adapted and survived the transition from the first to the second generations, sought solace and purpose in both American and Norwegian identities when faced with a collective sense of tragedy.

The news from Norway had left the Daughters of Norway delegates stunned, but it also filled the convention with resolve.[4] In her report from the meeting, which reads like a call to arms, Inga Frodesen recalled with horror the "beautiful valleys and open meadows" now turned into a battlefield. It "is painful to hear of it, and it is painful to read about this evil," she wrote, and insisted that "we have to take evil for what it is, and in earnest get on with it, if we are ever [again] to witness peace on earth."[5] Frodesen expressed a wish for women to abolish war altogether, but in the present tragedy called on her sisters to do their part to alleviate the suffering of their kindred folk in "the land from which we or our forebears came."[6]

The German invasion and occupation of Norway represented a moment of crisis experienced on both an individual level by those worrying about the well-being of relatives and friends, and on a collective level by a group experiencing shared suffering and worry. As such, this event, and World War II more generally, offers a unique window on the interplay between processes of assimilation and acculturation on the one hand, and retained ethnic and cultural distinction on the other. Assimilation has persisted as a governing concept in immigration historiography in the United States. Scholars have through much of the last half century moved away from the one-way assimilation model that once represented the only interpretive framework through which historians sought to understand the immigrant experience. While most migration scholars emphasize cultural pluralism and ethnic cultural survival in a multicultural transnational context, some, such as Elliott Barkan and Richard Alba, have continued to argue that the immigration experience should be understood as one of "integration" and "incorporation."[7]

Alba understands "assimilation" as adaptation and change in the immigrant community over time; a process of becoming American that both the Italian immigrants of the first decades of the twentieth century and contemporary migrants hold in common. He acknowledges that "assimilation" represents but one identifiable pattern of "immigrant-group incorporation in American society" that is not necessarily the dominant experience of a given ethnicity in a given historical context. To Alba, however, a clear conceptual lens of "assimilation" is necessary to detect some of the continuities that connect historical migrations to present-day ones.[8]

With his "new assimilation theory" in the 1980s, Alba maintained that World War II represented a turning point for the Italian-American ethnic community, in which largely second-generation Italian Americans demonstrated their willingness to make the ultimate sacrifice for their adopted country as government propaganda also minimized ethnic differences to highlight unity in the war effort. With World War II, Italian-American ethnicity had reached its twilight phase, he ventured, after which later generations held little connection to their ancestral homeland.[9] In comparison, Pacific Northwest Norwegians did not view their American and Norwegian identities as mutually exclusive, and subsequently simultaneous processes of acculturation and affirmation of cultural distinction can be seen at play in their reactions to World War II.

This essay responds in part to Roger Lotchin's call for more studies on Scandinavians (as well as a number of other neglected ethnic groups) on the American home front, and on the broader topic of ethnicity and war, along with Nancy Carnevale's indirect call for further study of ethnicity and language in the American immigrant community context.[10] It also engages with Gary Gerstle, who argues that World War II in some ways was indeed a "good war." In his examination of the European ethnic working class in the United States, Gerstle asserts that for these ethnics, World War II became "the historic moment when they felt fully accepted as Americans." According to Gerstle, ethnic workers sensed that the American dream was within their grasp, and subsequently—from their desire for recognition and acceptance as Americans—wholeheartedly adopted the nation's patriotism and became deeply engaged with the war.[11] While many Pacific Northwest Norwegians held working-class occupations in the shipping, fishing, and lumber industries, they had largely felt fully accepted in the American mainstream since the latter half of the nineteenth century.[12] Instead, the Nazi German occupation of Norway appears to have been a substantial factor in motivating patriotism among Pacific Northwest Norwegians. From a Norwegian-American perspective, the American war effort, its outcomes, and the involvement of their own people all truly represented a "good war" in which they made a contribution on behalf of both their countries. As a snapshot of a historic moment, then, the occupation highlights an ethnic community in crisis, but it also illuminates one firmly entrenched and flourishing in a multicultural society.

Many initially reacted to the German invasion of Norway with shock and grief, reaffirmation of Norwegianness, and resolve to act. In Seattle, when the news broke about German troops in his native Norway, University of Washington music professor August Werner had just received the joyous news that His Majesty King Haakon VII had bestowed upon him knighthood through the Order of St. Olav for his achievements representing Norway as a baritone, choir director, and teacher.[13] On May 17, while Norwegian, British, French, and Polish troops still fought the German invader in Norway, Werner delivered the first Norwegian-language keynote address in years at Seattle's annual celebration of the Norwegian Constitution Day in Civic Auditorium—a beautiful concert hall and convention center on the future grounds of the 1962 World's Fair and the Seattle Center. His lecture had been moved to the Auditorium from the smaller Masonic Temple due to an expected increase in attendance.[14] As people settled into their seats that evening, many of them no doubt glanced around the room. People had filled all the rows of seats, and by the time the program got started over two thousand had filled the gallery as well.[15] At eight o'clock the Concert Orchestra opened the festivities with an Edvard Grieg overture, followed by appropriate greetings from Chairman A. S. Ryland of the Seventeenth of May Committee. Then the Norwegian Male Chorus entered the stage. As the opening tones of the Norwegian national anthem played, the audience spontaneously rose to their feet and joined the choir in singing "*Ja, vi elsker dette landet*" (Yes, we love this country).

The full program included the presentation of the Order of St. Olav to Seattle mayor (and soon-to-be governor of Washington State) Arthur B. Langlie, and additional speeches in "well articulated English" by Langlie and the Reverend Trygve O. Svare, professor of religion at Pacific Lutheran College in Tacoma and future cultural attaché at the American embassy in Oslo. In addition, the event represented a musical expression of Norwegian heritage, collective memory, and cautious optimism that Norway once more would win its freedom, through a collection of Norwegian folk tunes performed by the Concert Orchestra and the Norwegian

Male Chorus under Werner's direction.[16] Werner's address, often interrupted by thundering applause, also dwelled on that same message. "I have always been proud to have been born a Norwegian," he told his audience near the end of his speech, "but I am most proud to be so at this time. And I will become prouder still in the days to come."[17] By the end of his delivery, the audience did not hesitate to grant his request of joining him in song: "*Gud signe vaart dyre fedreland*" (God bless our dear fatherland).[18]

Figure 1. August Werner (1893–1980). Courtesy of University of Washington Libraries, Special Collections, UW23862z.

Werner's speech reflected personal shock and disbelief, and his words struck a chord with the Pacific Northwest Norwegian audience who had turned out in force. He attempted to set a hopeful and prideful tone, but he also conveyed deep sadness. He opened by reminding his listeners that the Seventeenth of May was the greatest day of celebration for all Norwegians, but quickly moved on to the undeniable anguish of everyone present and the overarching topic of his address—the difficult situation in which he, his listeners, and all Norwegians now found themselves. While the Seventeenth of May celebration of freedom and independence had been a Norwegian nationalist symbol in Seattle since the 1890s, this particular Seventeenth of May was also "a dark, monstrous day of sorrow," according to Werner. "The Norwegian flags no longer fly in the wind," he said. "They no longer blush red in the spring sun." It was not just an issue of friends and relatives "suffering the terrors and desperations of war," he continued, but also "a whole nation's life and future . . . threatened by [a] barbaric, bestial tyranny."[19] These words surely resonated with an auditorium filled with likeminded people.

Others expressed shock and personal anguish in print publications. Roald Lund, a columnist for *Washington Posten,* wrote in his first post-invasion column that the "battles raging in and about Norway are no fiercer than those in the hearts of all Norwegian-Americans."[20] Marie Vognild Lund shared that sentiment, and felt she could "shed tears of blood." She wrote of all Daughters of Norway, stating: "our hearts bleed and our eyes are filled with tears by the thought of the injustice and barbarism that has afflicted our dear Norway."[21] Olav Gunheim remembered his school days in cities that he believed existed no longer. John Lund, editor of *Camas Post Record,* also remembered his time in Norway, including the six months he spent at the University of Oslo—his father's alma mater: "I have sailed the fjords and climbed the mountains where all was peace and beauty until the mad dictator of Germany rushed in with sudden death and destruction from bombs and high explosive shells to be followed by the dreaded agents of Gestapo."[22]

For many, the sorrow and heartache over Germany's occupation of Norway translated into fear and deep anxiety for the well-being of loved ones living in the war zone. They scrutinized newspapers for scattered information about conditions in Norway.[23] They also gathered with others in churches for "special prayers for Norway and its people."[24] Columnist Roald Lund wrote of the sharp, personal tragedy shared by all readers. Just ten days after the invasion, he wrote, "There are few of us who do not have immediate relatives in the war zone. And with one voice we ask 'where are they—how are they—why don't we hear from them—what can we do for them!' And the answer is as tragic as the questions: 'nobody knows.'"[25]

When a person did receive word from Norway the news contained in the letter held great public interest. The first such letter, published in February 1941 in *Dötre av Norge Paa Stillehavskysten,* the Daughters of Norway of the Pacific Coast's monthly newspaper, described hardship in Steinkjer, a small community in the province of Nord-Trøndelag. It detailed the fate of Steinkjer, including the author and his mother's flight and relocation some thirty kilometers away from town only a few days before its destruction. We "have lost everything of ours," the author confided, "apart from the clothes on our backs."[26] Another letter, part of which the newspaper published three months later, discussed a horrific battle in Gratangen in Northern Norway witnessed by the writer. She offered details of the battle, and its consequences for the locals, to her sister in Tacoma, Washington. A battalion of Norwegian soldiers from the Trøndelag provinces had sought refuge near the local farmhouses, when German troops came bearing down on them. Fortunately, no civilians were killed, but a few houses were burned down and locals had to bury thirty-two Trønder soldiers from the Norwegian battalion when the battle was over.[27]

In addition to the publishing of some letters in newspapers, other lucky recipients of word from friends and family shared them with relatives through the mail. Iver Klukken of Ferndale, Washington, was one such person. After he and other relatives in the United States sent repeated letters to his brother Mikal Kluken, a schoolteacher in a rural community in the mountains east of Trondheim, a response finally arrived some time during the winter or spring of 1941. Mikal wrote that as of January 1941, "we have thus far had sufficient food and clothing," referring to the topic twice and in obvious response to inquiries from his brother. Mikal did not have any great suffering to report regarding his immediate family, but conveyed a sense of inconvenience at his forced, though temporary, relocation. He also relayed an almost desperate need of getting away from it all at times, from "war, radio, telephone, and first and foremost, propaganda and agitation from the most conflicting of parties."[28] A letter that served more to calm his relatives' fears about the author's safety rather than as a call for help, it nevertheless caught the attention and imagination of worried expatriates in America. It made the rounds as a form of chain mail sent from one relative to another over the next year, from Washington to Minnesota and perhaps all the way to the East Coast, before it made its way back to Washington again. In response to receiving the letter, Anders Larsen wrote from somewhere in Minnesota: "In the times in which we now live—it is good that we can reach each other with letters as that is a great benefit that many cannot have."[29] Sigrid Kleiken also thanked Iver for sharing "the Norway-letter . . . which we all read with interest," and told him that "Anna sent it to Osakis [Minnesota] after it had been read by everyone here."[30] Anna, in turn, pointed out that Mikal had apparently "received one of the three [letters] I sent last fall," and that "you will soon have [the Norway-letter] back."[31] Such news from friends and family in Norway certainly calmed nerves, and offered supplemental information about conditions there from a trustworthy source, which undoubtedly inspired a greater desire to help in any which way possible amongst the recipients.

Shock and despair, along with worry on behalf of friends and relatives, quickly transitioned into a longer-term resolve and determination. Relief work gave Pacific Northwest Norwegians a purpose amid the worry and despair, and it promoted unity among them. As Gudrun Oustad mused at the time, "When a people suffer and worry they seem to become closer."[32] By July 1940, *Dötre av Norge Paa Stillehavskysten* carried reports that local lodges of Daughters of Norway had formed sewing and knitting societies and clubs and were hard at work making quality clothing by hand to ship to people in need in Norway.[33] Marie Berglund of Embla Lodge in Tacoma reported that their group met once a month in various members' homes for knitting. By November 1940, they had wrapped and shipped Christmas presents for the Norwegian airmen at Camp Little Norway in Canada. No matter the regional origin of the sisters, Berglund noted, "the great thing about the work of Daughters of Norway is that whether from the South, North, East or West of Norway [or from Wisconsin], we are united for one purpose: Promoting Daughters of Norway. Helping Norway has now been added" to that purpose.[34] In February 1941, Valkyrien Lodge of Seattle and Breidablik Lodge of Ballard reported their production to date of socks, sweaters, hats, mittens, nightgowns, and the like for adults and children came to a total of 421 items and 750 items respectively.[35]

In addition to women's clubs' knitting efforts, Pacific Northwest Norwegians also organized fundraisers for Norwegian relief. While some expressed concern that donations might benefit the Germans, the community nevertheless quickly organized to provide aid to Norway. Seattle's Leif Erikson Lodge of the Sons of Norway had a relief committee ready on April 10, 1940, to begin fundraising work on short notice.[36] The Royal Norwegian Legation in Washington, D.C., began to receive "unsolicited contributions from all parts of [the] country" in the first few days of the conflict.[37] *Washington Posten* reported that it was touching to witness all the forces in motion to help Norway: "By letter, telephone or in person the question posed is what is being done to help Norway, and how can I help?"[38] Columnist Roald Lund joined the call by asking all readers "to collect and send every possible cent to the Norwegian aid fund" and to do so "FOR YOUR RELATIVES."[39]

The Norwegian aid effort took center stage during Seventeenth of May festivities, as it did during other sponsored events throughout the year such as concerts or lectures. August Werner gave his time and effort "unselfishly . . . to further [Norwegian Relief's] work of succoring to the needs of our dear ones across the sea," in his many appearances as choir director or baritone.[40] Norwegian Relief, Inc., wasted no men, means, nor time in their "17th of May Crusade" for Norwegian Relief. Incorporated only a couple of weeks before May 17, 1940, the organization had sought to unify local Norwegian aid efforts around the country under its umbrella. Their State Department license provided legitimacy under which locals happily submitted. On and around the Constitution Day festivities of 1941, their well-marketed "Crusade" went highly noticed. The Seattle Seventeenth of May Committee printed Norwegian Relief's poster in full color on the front page of the event program, and placed enough posters around the Civic Center to attract attendees' attention. The "17th of May Crusade" poster—depicting a young Norwegian girl, arms raised as if expecting the assistance of an adult, standing in front of a full-color Norwegian flag at the bottom of which one can make out the smoldering ruins of a city—proved successful enough to warrant reuse in later years' programs. It was also used in newspapers to illustrate the work of Norwegian Relief at all times of the year and even after the organization's name had changed to American Relief for Norway.[41] Perhaps it was the irresistible eyes of the poster girl or community pressure and a wish to beat "the Joneses"; or perhaps it was a genuine desire to help the needy citizens of the country of one's parents' birth; whatever the individual reasons for lending a hand, donations poured into the Chicago central office of Norwegian Relief. The amount contributed had passed $250,000 by July 31, 1940, and while contributions slacked over the next few months—perhaps due to fears of aiding and comforting the enemy—they gradually picked up again and surpassed $520,000 by May 31, 1941.[42]

Local organizers wasted no time combining Norwegian Relief fundraising with lectures given by witnesses to "what had happened in Norway," who traveled around visiting Norwegian-American communities throughout the United States. In October 1940, Inga Frodesen of Valkyrien Lodge reported on the Seattle visits of three notable witnesses to the events that had unfolded in Norway. The first, Theodor Broch, the Mayor of Narvik, described the battle in which the Allies had successfully recaptured the city and driven the German troops in the area to the brink

Figure 2. Norwegian Relief poster, Seattle Seventeenth of May celebration, 1942. From the Esther Lund Nilsen Collection, World War II Scrapbooks, MSS 280, Box 1. Courtesy of Pacific Lutheran University Archives and Special Collections.

of surrender, when Prime Minister Churchill had reshuffled the deck by withdrawing the British troops. Elisabeth Prytz spoke of conditions in Norway up to the time of her departure in August 1940, and C. J. Hambro, president of the Norwegian parliament, gave his account of what had transpired in Norway in April 1940.[43] The Norwegian government-in-exile in London sponsored such speaking tours through their representative in Washington, D.C., which even included members of the royal family. Unsurprisingly, witness accounts made a significant impression on Norwegian-American communities in the Pacific Northwest and elsewhere. Lectures were always well attended by first- and second-generation immigrants hungry for reliable news from Norway. Speakers and representatives from the Norwegian government-in-exile acted on behalf of Norwegian Relief, but they also undoubtedly set out to present an official Norwegian narrative and to seek out public support in the United States.

In addition to clothing drives and fundraising, Norwegian fraternal organizations in the Pacific Northwest continued to pursue their objective of maintaining and protecting the Norwegian cultural heritage throughout the war. They prioritized the maintenance of the Norwegian language but this was not without its challenges. Not unlike Alba's Italian Americans, the Norwegian-American community in the Pacific Northwest had largely transitioned to the second generation by 1940. Most Norwegian migrants to the Pacific Northwest had arrived between the 1880s and the mid-1920s, and the Scandinavian population of Washington had surpassed that of any other non–Anglo Saxon ethnic group by 1890.[44] For the United States as a whole, Scandinavian immigration had peaked at sixty-five thousand a year in the 1880s, and declined to less than two thousand per year by the 1930s.[45] The war, however, led to a small increase in immigration numbers to five thousand annually, which continued into the 1950s.[46] The number of Norwegian-born migrants who made it to the Pacific Northwest after 1930, however, was small.

By 1944, Gyda Christoferson, the president of the Grand Lodge of the Daughters of Norway of the Pacific Coast, cited the continued use of the Norwegian language as one of the most important and yet most difficult tasks of the organization since further immigration seemed impossible.[47] Unlike Italian Americans' use of the Italian language during World War II, however, Norwegian Americans' use of the Norwegian language did not mark the ethnic community with suspicion. While the use of the Italian language was subject to scrutiny by the United States' government as a possible sign of disloyalty and a security threat, Norwegian Americans encountered little to no stigma or public ostracization as a result of their continued use of the Norwegian language.[48]

The founders of the fraternal organizations had deemed maintenance of the Norwegian language an important end goal, and recruitment an essential means. The German occupation of Norway made this task no less relevant during World War II. Carl Hansen of the Sons of Norway noted in 1940 that lodge after

Døtre av Norge

STILLEHAVS-KYSTEN

4. AARGANG | APRIL 1940 | NR. 4

Hilsen Til Dötre av Norge Paa Stillehavskysten

Av Inga Frodesen

Vi møttes, foreslo og kranglet litt i Portland, Ore. men vi skiltes som gode venner og med et ønske i vaart sinn, og det var, at freden maatte komme snart, og at alle mødres gutter maa få lov til aa føle sig trygge.

Vi talte, sang og bad for vårt eget moderland Norge, men vi tok alltid de andre lande med i vaar bøn, fordi vi vet at moderhjerte er det samme overalt, og at de gutter som maa ut for aa slaa ned, blir mordere imot sin vilje, de er kjære og uskyldige. Gud hjelpe dem! La underet skje, at der kan bli fred over hele verden og aldri, aldri mere krig!

Vi laget love for vaar orden og var ganske enige. Mange unge var kommet til møtet denne gang, især fra syden. De talte fritt og begeistret for Døtre av Norge og vilde staa frem for aa bygge op ordenen.

Portland hadde tatt sin vakreste vaardrakt paa og statens guvernør fortalte, at dette var gjort fordi vi skulde komme. — Baade den ærede guvernør og byens borgermester sa, at de følte slik sympati for oss og vaart folk under disse tider, og selv om de maatte være forsiktige i sine ord, saa lot de oss forstaa sine tanker.

La oss gratulere Portlands stævne-komite som maktet aa

Fra Vaar Nye Storlosjepresident

Anna Kolbjörnsen No. 4 San Francisco, Calif.

It has been "Quiet on our western front," and there is little to report besides the routine work of the lodge.

At our last meeting in March we had the pleasure of having five members of the Oakland chapter, Gjøa, as our guests: Mrs. Olga Johnson, vice-president of the Supreme Lodge, Mrs. Moran, Mrs. Berit Johnson, and Mrs. Beringer. Each one expressed a kind greeting, and it is our hope they will be with us often.

The last issue of "Daughters of Norway" was a treat with the photograps of our Supreme Officers. Actually seeing them face to face they seem nearer and a bit more real. The dear, familiar face of our own Mrs. Julin makes it even more so.

Thank you Mrs. Brochgrevink, for the delightful letters you have sent to our chapter. We deeply regret you cannot attend our meetings. Our best wishes for your good health. Write to us again, will you?

About seventy of our members attended the surprise shower given by our Past-president, Mrs. Petra Westre, at her home for one of our youngest members, Evelyn Dybdal. The guests all report a most enjoyable evening. Miss Dybdal received so many gifts, both practical and beautiful. At our last regular meeting we were all invited to attend her wedding, April 8. From us all sincere wishes for the happiest of mar-

Figure 3. Newly elected Grand Lodge president Gyda Christoferson, 1940. *Dötre av Norge Paa Stillehavskysten* 4:4 (April 1940): 1. Courtesy of Pacific Lutheran University Archives and Special Collections.

lodge had become English-speaking, despite the organization's original objective "to maintain and further interest in the Norwegian language and whatever is good and noble in the Norwegian national character." He concluded, however, that the use of English to promote the Norwegian language and culture amongst the younger generation was a benefit rather than a hindrance, and that "those of the younger generation who have joined our ranks have done so because they possess the pride of race and believe that the homeland of their fathers has given to the world cultural values worthy of preservation."[49] Hansen's belief that there had been an uptick in interest in his organization—in its values and its work—fits the experience of Seattle's Leif Erikson Lodge, which announced its recent strong recruitment numbers in November 1940.[50] By 1943, Tordenskjold Lodge's total recruitment in and around Spokane, Washington, exceeded that of any other chapter in the country. The lodge had experienced substantial growth since 1941, and in acknowledgment of the Spokane chapter's feat in reaching a membership of one thousand, Sons of Norway president Erick Bjarne Hauke made the trip from Minneapolis to personally admit the batch of members that officially made Tordenskjold Lodge the largest chapter in the country.[51]

Daughters of Norway numbers also provided grounds for some optimism. Gyda Christoferson noted in 1944 that Camilla Collett Lodge of Silvana, Washington, had doubled its membership in recent years, and that all other lodges had added members as well, but that increasing numbers of new members did not speak Norwegian.[52] Two years earlier, she had mused that the order could only survive long term with the recruitment of young people. She maintained that they "must not abandon the Norwegian language since it is at the heart of Daughters of Norway," but suggested a middle road. "Why can't the young learn Norwegian from us, and we learn English from them?"[53]

While some lodges of the Daughters of Norway had switched to English as their language of business by World War II, all lodges supported efforts to promote the language. Every year, for example, the Grand Lodge sponsored a high school Norwegian-language essay contest, and awarded a scholarship to the winner, as well as a cash prize to the runner-up. In 1941, Muriel Baird of Stadium High School in Tacoma won the scholarship for her essay on Norway, Norwegian life, and Norwegian culture.[54] The next year, Ethel Hansen of Ballard High School won with an essay on the people who have made Norway best known.[55] And in 1943, Kenneth Rasmussen of North Kitsap High School in Poulsbo, Washington, received the scholarship with his essay on the topic "Norway's contribution to the war effort in the last world war."[56] By 1944, however, only Everett High School still offered instruction in Norwegian, so the scholarship prizes were awarded to the student in that program that excelled the most.[57] Despite the efforts of the older generations to promote instruction in the language, and the use of the language in their fraternity organization work, the transition to a predominantly second generation left its mark on the community. Betty Lingen, the recipient of a 1942 university scholarship, submitted a letter of gratitude in English because she was unable to transcribe her letter into a Norwegian that "satisfied either my mother or myself."

She promised enrollment in a Scandinavian course next quarter, since she had prioritized first aid training in the present term.[58]

Apart from linguistic challenges, there was broad consensus on the necessity and importance of preserving Norwegian cultural heritage throughout the war, particularly since the source of this heritage suffered under a German yoke. Gudrun Oustad, for example, found that shared suffering and worry held a unifying quality. It drew Pacific Northwest Norwegians closer. She took some comfort in this realization in the summer of 1940. "We are inclined to take things for granted," she wrote, "but if we find that our values are in danger, they become very important to us. We are proud to know that the Norwegian history, art and literature are still existing in the world today and will continue to do so."[59] Marie Vognild Lund recalled the founders' vision:

> To unite Norwegian-American women in sisterhood for the purpose of maintaining common memories and traditions. To honor Mother Norway by demonstrating high ideals, by bringing out the best in our people's character [ethnic traits], and by so doing becoming better citizens of our adopted country. Always ready to support a cause for the improvement of our people, and at the very least, to seek out the best way of bringing our inheritance to the next generation. . . . Sons and Daughters of Norway stand guard over everything Norwegian, a new aspect of our mission, to watch over all these heirlooms and maintain our love of it all until Norway once again stands saved and free.[60]

This rhetoric is common in Seventeenth of May speeches, editorials, letters to the editor, and poetry published in *Washington Posten* and *Dötre av Norge Paa Stillehavskysten* throughout the war, as well as in letters and notes left by August Werner and others. This rhetoric does not represent a departure from the past, but a continuation into the World War II era of ideas and values, and efforts made over several decades—efforts made especially pertinent after 1940 in the context of the

German occupation of Norway, and the declining percentage of first-generation immigrants among Norwegian Americans.

In addition to the efforts of *Washington Posten* and the local chapters of fraternal organizations to promote Norwegian language and culture in the Pacific Northwest, Norwegian-American organizations, broadly speaking, held influence over local efforts as well. *Det Norske Selskab i Amerika*—the Norwegian Society of America—for example, had worked for the preservation and promotion of Norwegian culture in America since its founding in 1903. Organized by highly educated immigrants living around Eau Claire, Wisconsin, and Minneapolis and Northfield, Minnesota, the organization also drew membership from the Pacific Northwest as early as 1903.[61] *Det Norske Selskab i Amerika*'s Sigvald Quale Memorial Contest—a "declamation competition" in schools across Norwegian America—took shape in the 1910s. In Poulsbo, Washington, Arnt Oyen, a local schoolteacher, organized Quale contests in the 1940s.[62] According to *Washington Posten,* the March 6, 1942, declamation competition in Poulsbo represented the fifth Quale contest held by the students in the Norwegian class at the local high school. In that competition, students recited stories, fairytales, and songs in the Norwegian language. The pronunciation might not be as perfect as the reader might remember from childhood, the newspaper mused, but nevertheless posited that the event still promised to spark cherished childhood memories desperately needed at a time of limited contact with Norway on account of the war. *Washington Posten* also highlighted a "curiosity" with the 1942 contest: "One of the students is an Indian. And what is strange is that his Norwegian pronunciation is better in many situations than any of those who knew some Norwegian when they started last fall. The Indian has the piece 'Smørbukk' on the program, and will no doubt earn much praise."[63] Dave Adams, the Indian boy, earned fourth place, but according to Valborg Ager, Oyen felt that he should have placed third.[64] With the support of local chapters of Daughters and Sons of Norway, then, as well as programs of national reach such as the Quale contest, Pacific Northwest school teachers taught Norwegian language and culture to students of Norwegian-American ancestry, as well as others, and thereby made a contribution to the preservation of this cultural heritage among the younger generations, even during World War II.

The Japanese assault on Pearl Harbor made no less impact on Pacific Northwest Norwegians than the German invasion of Norway. Gyda Christoferson offered a response in the December 1941 issue of *Dötre av Norge Paa Stillehavskysten*:

> The thing that we had hoped would never come to our shores has come, war. War that can only bring tears and heartaches and sorrow into many lives and many homes. War that takes the best we have to give, our youth. War, that spells misery and destruction to civilians as well as men in uniforms. War, that brings hatred into human hearts. But now, when it has come, let us face it with the same courage and the same determination that the peoples of the old world have faced it now for years.[65]

Christoferson most commonly wrote in Norwegian, so her choice of voicing her reaction to the entry of the United States into the war in English suggests a desire on her part, or perhaps as expected on the part of her readers, to express American identity (and sympathy) at a time of crisis for the United States. Stjernen Lodge of Astoria, Oregon, chimed in that in these troubling times "[we] can only hope and believe that our country and the dear little Norway will emerge in good health from this war."[66]

Washington Posten noted the similarities between Nazi Germany's sneak attack on Norway and the Japanese sneak attack on Pearl Harbor, and emphasized that the United States and Norway now were allies. "By arriving in this way, [the attack] left no room for doubt or disagreement as to the course America should take. The country stood at once in full agreement over the only possible course of action," O. L. Ejde wrote in his editorial in the December 12, 1941, issue of *Washington Posten*—the first after the December 7 attack.[67] When Wilhelm Morgenstierne, the representative of the Norwegian government-in-exile to the United States, noted that the United States and Norway now stood "shoulder to shoulder" having both experienced the treachery of an unprovoked sneak attack, few, if any, disagreed.[68] *Washington Posten*'s first editorial after December 7 compared Hawaii to Norway. "Many ridiculed and condemned Norway's defense at the time for incompetence and idiocy. . . . After the drama at Pearl Harbor the events of that April night are more understandable. In Europe a small country . . . became prey . . . for a new style of warfare."[69] Nazi Germany had preyed upon Norway with a sneak attack, and now the United States experienced the same destruction. The focus, among Norwegian Americans and Americans alike, had shifted overnight. The United States was no longer neutral. The United States was at war, and it had allies in that struggle. One of these allies was Norway, identified shortly after Pearl Harbor by President Roosevelt as a valuable ally in the struggle ahead.[70]

The life and work of Pacific Northwest Norwegians, and their organizations, experienced both change and continuity on account of the involvement of the United States in the war. The changes were no more dramatic for Pacific Northwest Norwegians than they were for most other Americans. The various sewing and knitting societies of the Daughters of Norway of the Pacific Coast quickly transitioned their labor to benefit the American Red Cross.[71] Norwegian Relief became American Relief for Norway, Inc., in 1942, to accommodate requests from the President's War Relief Control Board to emphasize its "Americanness," mainly so recipients of aid would know where the aid came from.[72]

Hannah Oas of Thelma Lodge in Everett, Washington, reminded her sisters that "[one] thing . . . should be uppermost in our minds—how we Daughters of Norway can best serve America as true American citizens," but she also noted that they still ought to make plans "for the future help of our people in Norway when the time comes that our Norwegian flag will again unfurl and fly freely over a free people in a free Norway."[73] In May 1942, Normanna Lodge of the Sons of Norway of Everett and Thelma Lodge of the Daughters of Norway unveiled the theme for the Twenty-Third Biennial Convention: "Our Contribution to the Cause of Freedom." The Everett convention hosts further posited that "[we] can most truly reflect the tradition of freedom handed down to us by our forefathers in Norway, by pledging anew our love for and allegiance to the United States of America and the lofty ideals for which it stands."[74] In an environment saturated with American patriotism, it is no surprise that members of ethnic organizations also expressed American patriotism. Without a doubt, to both the Sons and Daughters of Norway, the American patriotism they expressed was heartfelt.

The key change, for Pacific Northwest Norwegians and for all other Americans, is of course that after December 7, 1941, members of their own community enlisted and went to war. Unsurprisingly, *Washington Posten* now began to showcase Norwegian-American servicemen in the United States military. Coupled with news on the American war effort in general, this news coverage probably reflected community interest rather than a conscious demonstration of American loyalty on the part of the newspaper. Individual officers' appointments or promotion to higher rank, letters from servicemen, and the occasional obituary to a fallen hero all found their place in *Washington Posten.*[75] While servicemen undoubtedly usually thought of loved ones when they found time to write letters, some occasionally wrote to *Washington Posten* as well. Private Olaf Boe, for example, wrote from Camp Hale, Colorado, where he received training as a mountain ski trooper. When "a Norwegian company from Minnesota" came to join them for training in wintry mountain conditions, Norwegians across units engaged in these activities "with spirited eagerness," he reported. On Christmas, they held a Norwegian service, "which brought memories back to our dear country that we are now longing to fight for," he continued, before finishing his letter with a reiteration of his hope that they would soon face the enemy, and a request for more copies of *Washington Posten* to please the men of Camp Hale.[76] No doubt American patriots, the Norwegian-American soldiers of Camp Hale also expressed Norwegian patriotism. When calls first came for Norwegian Americans to join the 99th Battalion—an infantry unit of Norwegian speakers trained for mountain and winter warfare—the newspaper, along with many Norwegian Americans, had initially reacted with puzzlement. Upon realizing that the organization of this unit was not a slight on Norwegian Americans' English skills, but rather evidence that "America imagines the possibility of requiring Norwegian-speaking soldiers" in the field, *Washington Posten* found the existence of this unit both inspiring and encouraging.[77] "Anyone can understand where such [soldiers] are most likely to be found useful," the newspaper mused, and continued following the unit's movements with interest until the end of the war.[78]

American patriotism on the part of Pacific Northwest Norwegians did not prevent continued expressions of Norwegian identity, nor did it preclude continued work for the preservation of Norwegian cultural heritage and fundraising for Norwegian Relief. Stjernen Lodge of Astoria, Oregon, announced in 1942 that they planned a combined "17th of May Festival and 'I am an American Day,'" asserting both American patriotism and Norwegian identity.[79] Along with the Seventeenth of May, remembrances of the more infamous April 9, 1940, also occurred. In 1943, for example, the Norwegian community in Seattle held a fundraising rally "for Norway's cause" at the Masonic Temple with music and speeches framing an event that resembled a Seventeenth of May celebration, "only difference being that everybody spoke Norwegian except August Werner."[80]

The Seventeenth of May celebrations in Seattle in the years 1942 to 1945—though moved back to the smaller Masonic Temple—took on similar formats as in the past and continued to sponsor Norwegian Relief with their proceeds. In both 1942 and 1943, the Seventeenth of May Committee reminded their patrons that "Norway needs your help today" through the irresistible eyes of the Norwegian Relief girl and August Werner's musical arrangements.[81] *Dötre av Norge Paa Stillehavskysten* gave the first extensive update on the clothing drive for Norwegian Relief in November 1942, following the previous report in June 1941. Norwegian Aid in Seattle reported that they had 3,026 articles of new woolen and cotton clothing on hand, and 3,677 articles of used woolen, cotton, and silk clothing.[82] In February 1943, the newspaper shared the news that ninety crates of new and used clothing bound for Norway was finally about to be shipped from Seattle.[83] In her report in connection with the 1942 convention in Everett, Gyda Christoferson reported that the Daughters of Norway had made their own donations and undertaken fundraisers for Norwegian Relief. Immediately after the United States' entry into the war, they had sent a telegram to President Roosevelt offering their support, and they had immediately begun work for the Red Cross. "Daughters of Norway is now everywhere helping where it is needed to win peace and victory for America and freedom for our dear Norway," she asserted. To Christoferson, one did not preclude the other. It was possible to work for both American victory and Norwegian freedom from the Nazi yoke at the same time.

By the time the Tordenskjold Lodge of the Sons of Norway invited delegates to the Twenty-Fourth Biennial Convention in Spokane, Washington, in 1944,

Washington Posten still published a weekly newspaper in Norwegian for its Pacific Northwest readership; *Dötre av Norge Paa Stillehavskysten* maintained its Norwegian name, and it continued to publish content in both Norwegian and English; and members of Daughters of Norway expressed a sense of pride in the humanitarian work that, according to Gyda Christoferson, made their organization respected everywhere.[84] By 1944, the various lodges of the Daughters of Norway of the Pacific Coast had raised funds for the Red Cross, Norwegian Relief, Camp Little Norway, Norwegian Seamen, Hospitality House, United Service Organizations (USO), Civilian Defense, Community Chest, War Chest, and War Bonds.[85] In addition to the challenges and successes various lodges met in connection to recruitment and use of the Norwegian language, these acts of financial support were among the achievements Christoferson reported on at the convention. As they thought back to the conventions of 1940 and 1942, the delegates undoubtedly felt a sense of continuity. Looking forward to the next convention in 1946, they departed Spokane with "renewed interest and strength to work together as Daughters of Norway, in the labors that will bring peace to our country, America—and help to our mother country, Norway."[86]

The celebration of the Seventeenth of May also continued to serve as an expression of Norwegian identity and a vehicle for commemorating and maintaining Norwegian heritage for the duration of the war. As the main speaker of the 1943 event, Governor Arthur B. Langlie looked out on a full auditorium when he spoke of "our" many celebrations over the years, and made his audience appreciate "the state governor [embodying] the role as one of us."[87] A second-generation Pacific Northwest Norwegian, Langlie not only exemplified the prominence to which individual Pacific Northwest Norwegians could aspire in the United States, but he continued to firmly identify himself as an active member of the Norwegian community in Seattle. Two years later, again to a filled house, August Werner stood on the same podium. When the celebration for which "every one of us have longed for five long years," had finally arrived, Werner's speech fittingly set the tone as it also had done five years prior. "Never before," *Washington Posten* commented, "has an occasion [more closely] fit his [loud] enthusiasm for all things Norwegian than this [particular] celebration."[88]

In the case of the Pacific Northwest Norwegians during World War II, then, was their experience primarily one of assimilation or cultural retention? Originally discredited due to its inherent one-directionality and ethnocentrism, the assimilation model redefined by Alba, Barkan, and others into a "new assimilation theory" does apply in part. Pacific Northwest Norwegians of the World War II era certainly believed they were becoming, or had become, American; and—to borrow an idea from Barkan—their ethnic group as a whole had started to move from the third to the fourth stage of Barkan's six-step model of ethnicity, which ranged from contact to assimilation.[89] By 1940, there were considerably more native-born than foreign-born Pacific Northwest Norwegians, the third and even fourth generations had emerged, there was substantial use of English among the later generations, and ethnic organizations made adjustments to maintain influence across generations. While the American patriotism spurred on by the war contributed in part toward accelerated Americanization, as it had during World War I, the German occupation of Norway bolstered Pacific Northwest Norwegians' Norwegian identities, at least to an extent. To Pacific Northwest Norwegians, their Norwegianness and Americanness were not mutually exclusive. It was not an either/or question. The war motivated efforts to protect and safeguard a Norwegian cultural heritage they perceived to be under threat from German machine guns rather than their own assimilation. Remaining first-generation immigrants possessed memories of pre-Nazi Norway, and the war made them more acutely aware that they possessed a heritage that was dear to them. World War II certainly boosted Norwegian identities in America, but the Norwegian-American institutions of the Pacific Northwest and elsewhere did not depend on that boost to survive. Norwegian Americans had already rooted their institutions in the Pacific Northwest and elsewhere well before the war. Neither wartime American loyalty nor bolstered Norwegian identities did much to affect the foothold of those institutions going into the 1950s and beyond.

Hans-Petter Grav *earned an MA from Montana State University in 2010, and a PhD from Washington State University in 2018. His research interests in Norwegian-American identity production in the Pacific Northwest took shape under the guidance of Dr. Robert Campbell at MSU Bozeman and Dr. Laurie Mercier at WSU Vancouver.*

NOTES

1. "Melding om dötre av Norges 22de Storlosjemöte i Portland, Ore. 1940," *Washington Posten,* April 19, 1940, 3. "Dötre av Norges Storlosjemöte i Portland, Oregon, 1940," *Dötre av Norge Paa Stillehavskysten* 4:4 (April 1940): 4.
2. "Hilsen Til Dötre av Norge Paa Stillehavskysten," *Dötre av Norge Paa Stillehavskysten* 4:4 (April 1940): 1, 2.
3. "Melding om dötre av Norges 22de Storlosjemöte I Portland, Ore. 1940," *Washington Posten,* April 19, 1940, 3. "Dötre av Norges Storlosjemöte I Portland, Oregon, 1940," *Dötre av Norge Paa Stillehavskysten* 4:4 (April 1940): 4. Norway unsuccessfully sought independence at the end of the Napoleonic wars. A Constitutional Assembly, however, nevertheless successfully hammered out a constitution inspired by the French and American revolutions, and their oath "Enige og tro til Dovre faller"—United and faithful until the Dovre mountains fall—became a nationalist symbol.
4. "Anna Kolbjörnsen Nr. 4 San Francisco, Cal.," *Dötre av Norge Paa Stillehavskysten* 4:5 (May 1940): 1.
5. "Hilsen Til Dötre av Norge Paa Stillehavskysten," *Dötre av Norge Paa Stillehavskysten* 4:4 (April 1940): 1, 2.
6. Phrase quoted from the convention resolutions, which reflects the collective view of Norway as communicated to people outside their organization. The phrase is not necessarily Frodesen's own words. *Dötre av Norge Paa Stillehavskysten* 4:4 (April 1940): 4.
7. See Elliott R. Barkan, "Immigration, Incorporation, Assimilation, and the Limits of Transnationalism: Introduction," *Journal of American Ethnic History* 25:2/3 (Winter/Spring 2006): 7–32; and Elliott R. Barkan, Hasia Diner, and Alan M. Kraut, eds., *From Arrival to Incorporation: Migrants to the U.S. in a Global Era* (New York, 2008). For a historiographical review essay on assimilation as an analytical concept in American ethnic history, see Russell A. Kazal, "Revisiting Assimilation: The Rise, Fall, and Reappraisal of a Concept in American Ethnic History," *American Historical Review* 100:2 (April 1995): 437–71.
8. Richard Alba and Victor Nee, *Remaking the American Mainstream: Assimilation and Contemporary Immigration* (Cambridge, Mass., 2003), x-xi.
9. Peter Kivisto, "The Origins of 'New Assimilation Theory,'" *Ethnic and Racial Studies* 40:9 (2017): 1418–29.
10. See Roger W. Lotchin, "The Historians' War or the Home Front's War?: Some Thoughts for Western Historians," *Western Historical Quarterly* 26:2 (Summer 1995): 188–89; and Nancy C. Carnevale, "'No Italian Spoken for the Duration of the War': Language, Italian-American Identity, and Cultural Pluralism in the World War II Years," *Journal of American Ethnic History* 22:3 (Spring 2003): 5.
11. Gary Gerstle, "The Working Class Goes to War," chapter 4 in Lewis A. Erenberg and Susan E. Hirsch, eds., *The War in American Culture: Society and Consciousness during World War II* (Chicago, 1996), 112–21. There is a historiographical debate on the validity or invalidity of the notion of World War II from the U.S. perspective as a "good war." For a historiographical overview on the topic, see this same chapter. See also his chapter 5, "Good War, Race War, 1941–1945," in Gary Gerstle, *American Crucible: Race and Nation*

in the Twentieth Century (Princeton, N.J., 2001), 187–237, for more on this topic. Gerstle maintains that World War II represented a moment of true mainstream acceptance (not just believed on the part of the ethnics). Philip Gleason, on the other hand, argues that while liberals and intellectuals framed their message to the public in the language of cultural pluralism and diversity, this message was nevertheless "strongly assimilationist" in that it seemed motivated by unity and consensus as a remedy to fears of intergroup unrest. See Philip Gleason, "Americans All: World War II and the Shaping of American Identity," *Review of Politics* 43:4 (Oct. 1981): 503.

12. For more details on the Norwegian-American "settlement" of the Pacific Northwest, and ethnic and racial identity construction in that context, see my dissertation *Vesterheim in Red, White and Blue: The Hyphenated Norwegian-American and Regional Identity in the Pacific Northwest, 1890–1950,* chapters 1 and 2.
13. Kgl. Norsk Legasjon, Washington, D.C., to Werner, 5 April 1940, in August Werner Papers, Special Collections, University of Washington Libraries. Royal Norwegian Consulate, Seattle, to Werner, 26 April 1940, in August Werner Papers, Special Collections, University of Washington Libraries.
14. National days are an important means of imagining and inventing the nation, and also a useful vehicle for expatriates in claiming continued membership in the imagined community of the mother country. See Benedict Anderson, *Imagined Communities: Reflections on the Origin and Spread of Nationalism* (London/New York, 1991), 6–7; and David McCrone and Gayle McPherson, eds., *National Days: Constructing and Mobilising National Identity* (Hampshire/New York, 2009), xiii, 1–8. On the Seventeenth of May (Norwegian Constitution Day), see also my dissertation *Vesterheim in Red, White and Blue: The Hyphenated Norwegian-American and Regional Identity in the Pacific Northwest, 1890–1950,* chapter 3.
15. "Seattles 17 Mai Verdig Og Vakker Tale Paa Norsk Med Klang Og To I," *Washington Posten,* May 24, 1940, 6.
16. 17th of May Program, Civic Auditorium, Seattle, May 17, 1940, in August Werner Papers, Special Collections, University of Washington Libraries.
17. "17de mai, 1940," typewritten speech manuscript, May 17, 1940, in August Werner Papers, Special Collections, University of Washington Libraries.
18. "Seattles 17 Mai Verdig Og Vakker Tale Paa Norsk Med Klang Og To I," *Washington Posten,* May 24, 1940, 6.
19. "17de mai, 1940," August Werner Papers, Special Collections, University of Washington Libraries.
20. "Roald Lund's Column: The War in Norway," *Washington Posten,* April 12, 1940, 1.
21. "Brev fra fru Lund," *Dötre av Norge Paa Stillehavskysten* 4:5 (May 1940): 2, 4.
22. "Folk Skriver Om Krigen: Plyndringen Av Norge," *Washington Posten,* April 26, 1940, 3.
23. Knut Lykke to Ivar Lykke, 26 May 1940, in Ivar Lykke Papers, Archives and Manuscripts, Norwegian University of Science and Technology Gunnerus Library.
24. "Norway's Cause," advertisement, *Washington Posten,* April 12, 1940, 6. "Staa Norge Bi," *Washington Posten,* April 19, 1940, 5.
25. "Roald Lund's Column: Organize for Norway and Our People," *Washington Posten,* April 19, 1940, 1.
26. "Brev Fra Steinkjer," *Dötre av Norge Paa Stillehavskysten* 5:2 (February, 1941): 4.

27. "Av Et Norges-Brev," *Dötre av Norge Paa Stillehavskysten* 5:5 (May, 1941): 3.
28. Mikal Kluken, Verdal, to Iver J. Kluken, 8 Jan. 1941, in Iver J. Klukken Papers, Special Collections, University of Washington Libraries.
29. Anders Larsen to Iver J. Klukken, 19 Jan. 1942, in Iver J. Klukken Papers, Special Collections, University of Washington Libraries.
30. Mrs. John Kleiken, Eden, to Iver J. Klukken, 10 Feb. 1942, in Iver J. Klukken Papers, Special Collections, University of Washington Libraries.
31. Anna and Carl to Iver J. Klukken, undated, in Iver J. Klukken Papers, Special Collections, University of Washington Libraries.
32. "Dear Book-Lovers," *Dötre av Norge Paa Stillehavskysten* 4:8 (August 1940): 2.
33. "Valkyrien Nr. 1, D. av N. Sy- og Strikkeforening for Norges-Hjelpen," *Dötre av Norge Paa Stillehavskysten* 4:7 (July 1940): 1, 3.
34. "Fra Tacoma, Wash.," *Dötre av Norge Paa Stillehavskysten* 4:11 (November 1940): 2.
35. "Fra Losje Valkyrien Seattle, Wash.," and "Fra Breidablik Losje Seattle, Wash.," *Dötre av Norge Paa Stillehavskysten* 5:2 (February 1941): 2.
36. "Losje Leif Erikson Organiserer Hjelpekomite," *Washington Posten,* April 12, 1940, 6.
37. "Legasjonen Telegraferer," *Washington Posten,* April 12, 1940, 1.
38. "Norge Trenger Hjelp Og Hjelpen Skall Komme," *Washington Posten,* April 19, 1940, 1.
39. "Roald Lund's Column: Organize for Norway and Our People," *Washington Posten,* April 19, 1940, 1.
40. "Norwegian Male Chorus of Seattle," concert program, Benson Polytechnic School Auditorium, Portland, Oregon, Nov. 16, 1940, in August Werner Papers, Special Collections, University of Washington Libraries.
41. "17th of May Crusade," Norwegian Relief poster, undated, and "17th of May Festival Program," 1941, 1942, 1943, in August Werner Papers, Special Collections, University of Washington Libraries.
42. A. N. Rygg, *American Relief for Norway: A Survey of American Relief Work for Norway during and after the Second World War* (Chicago, 1947), 15–18.
43. "Fra Valkyrien Nr. 1 Seattle, Wash.," *Dötre av Norge Paa Stillehavskysten* 4:10 (October 1940): 2.
44. Carlos A. Schwantes, *The Pacific Northwest* (Lincoln, Neb., 1996), 229.
45. Carl L. Bankston III and Danielle Antoinette Hidalgo, eds., *Immigration in U S. History: Vol. 2* (Pasadena, Calif., 2006), 631. The number represents the Scandinavian immigrant total for the United States as a whole. Scandinavia is composed of Norway, Sweden, and Denmark.
46. Bankston III and Hidalgo, eds., 631.
47. "Storlosjepresidentens Rapport," *Dötre av Norge Paa Stillehavskysten* 8:6 (June 1944): 1.
48. Nancy C. Carnevale, "'No Italian Spoken for the Duration of the War': Language, Italian-American Identity, and Cultural Pluralism in the World War II Years," *Journal of American Ethnic History* 22:3 (Spring 2003): 3–4.
49. "The Norwegian Language," *Duluth Skandinav og Superior Tidende,* extra, May 17, 1940, 17.
50. "Leif Erikson Sönner Av Norge I God Vekst," *Washington Posten,* Nov. 22, 1940, 6.
51. "Tordenskjold I Spokane Er Nu Landets Störste Sönner av Norge Losje," *Washington Posten,* Oct. 29, 1943, 1.

52. “Storlosjepresidentens Rapport,” *Dötre av Norge Paa Stillehavskysten* 8:6 (June 1944): 1.
53. “Storlosjepresidentens Rapport,” *Dötre av Norge Paa Stillehavskysten* 6:6 (June 1942): 1, 3.
54. “Stilen Om Norge Som Vant Stipendiet,” *Dötre av Norge Paa Stillehavskysten* 5:8 (August 1941): 2.
55. “Hvem har gjort Norges navn best kjent?” *Dötre av Norge Paa Stillehavskysten* 6:6 (June 1942): 3.
56. “Storlosjens Stipendium,” *Dötre av Norge Paa Stillehavskysten* 7:6 (June 1943): 1.
57. “Storlosjepresidentens Rapport,” *Dötre av Norge Paa Stillehavskysten* 8:6 (June 1944): 1.
58. Editorial page, *Dötre av Norge Paa Stillehavskysten* 6:9 (September 1942): 2.
59. “Dear Book-Lovers,” *Dötre av Norge Paa Stillehavskysten* 4:8 (August 1940): 2.
60. “Storlosjen Dötre av Norge paa Pacific Kysten Gjennem 33 Aar,” *Dötre av Norge Paa Stillehavskysten* 5:3 (March 1941): 1–2.
61. Membership lists, 1903–1924, in Det Norske Selskap Papers, Norwegian-American Historical Association, Northfield, Minnesota.
62. Arnt Oyen to J. Jørgen Thompson, Jan. 15, 1940, and J. Jørgen Thompson to Arnt Oyen, Jan 25, 1940, in Det Norske Selskap Papers, Norwegian-American Historical Association, Northfield, Minnesota.
63. “Poulsbo Har Igjen Deklamasjons-Fest,” *Washington Posten,* Mar. 6, 1942, clipping in Det Norske Selskap Papers, Norwegian-American Historical Association, Northfield, Minnesota. “Smørbukk” is a Norwegian folktale collected by Asbjørnsen and Moe, first published in a series of pamphlets between 1841 and 1844. Smørbukk, which literally translates to “butter-buck” had long before the 1940s become a cultural icon and image of a well-fed, folksy, rural commoner. The character in the fairytale uses his wit to overcome three kidnappings where a troll woman intends to cook him into soup. A gruesome tale to say the least; the troll woman’s daughter becomes soup instead, and the tale ends with the death of the troll woman.
64. Valborg H. Ager to J. Jørgen Thompson, Mar. 16, 1942, in Det Norske Selskap Papers, Norwegian-American Historical Association, Northfield, Minnesota. Oyen continued to correspond with Professor Thompson of St. Olaf College and the Norwegian Society on the topic of declamation competitions throughout the war. See for example Arnt Oyen to J. Jørgen Thompson, Nov. 25, 1944, in Det Norske Selskap Papers, Norwegian-American Historical Association, Northfield, Minnesota.
65. “Greetings from Our Grand President,” *Dötre av Norge Paa Stillehavskysten* 5:12 (December 1941): 8.
66. “From Stjernen No. 7 Astoria, Oregon,” *Dötre av Norge Paa Stillehavskysten* 6:1 (January 1942): 1.
67. “Krigen,” *Washington Posten,* Dec. 12, 1941, 2. Mrs. Gunnar Lund—Marie Vognild Lund that is—served as publisher of *Washington Posten* after her husband’s death in 1940 and into 1943, when she herself passed away. Gunnar Lund had married Marie Vognild in 1900, and later made a long career as publisher and editor of *Washington Posten* from 1905 and up to his death.
68. “Shoulder to Shoulder!” *Superior Tidende,* Dec. 26, 1941, 3.
69. “Krigen,” *Washington Posten,* Dec. 12, 1941, 2.
70. “What Now that Our Country Is at War?” *Washington Posten,* Dec. 19, 1941, 1.

71. “Fra Losje Embla Nr. 2 Tacoma, Wash.,” *Dötre av Norge Paa Stillehavskysten* 6:2 (February 1942): 3.
72. Rygg, 45.
73. “Greetings from Sister Hannah Oas,” *Dötre av Norge Paa Stillehavskysten* 6:2 (February 1942): 4.
74. “Our Contribution to the Cause of Freedom (Our Convention Theme),” *Dötre av Norge Paa Stillehavskysten* 6:5 (May 1942): 1.
75. When the U.S. Army Air Corp promoted Philip Hauge, formerly a professor at Pacific Lutheran College in Tacoma, to the rank of captain, the newspaper took note. Oscar Eng’s appointment as captain in the U.S. Army Air Transportation Service, and subsequent promotion to major, also received attention. Portrait photographs accompanied occasional notes of fallen soldiers, though such reports were not common. For examples, see: “Hauge Ble Kaptein,” *Washington Posten,* Jan. 29, 1943, 1; “Kapt. Eng Blir Transport-Sjef,” *Washington Posten,* Oct. 9, 1942, 1; “Der Er Igjen Forfremmelser I Eng-Familien,” *Washington Posten,* Nov. 6, 1942, 6; and “Löytn. Haakenstad Er Falt I Afrika,” *Washington Posten,* Jan. 29, 1943, 1.
76. “Soldater-Brev,” *Washington Posten,* Jan. 15, 1943, 4. Norwegian Americans did not exclusively train for, or battle in, the European theater of war. Major Einar Prestrud wrote a series of letters to the editor (whom he called his friend) from the Pacific theater. See “But the Major Had Much Rather Have Fiskesuppe,” *Washington Posten,* Sep. 10, 1943, 1; and “The Major Needs a Good Cook,” *Washington Posten,* Apr. 7, 1944, 4.
77. Despite the suspicion with which the federal government viewed the use of the Italian language in the United States, Nancy Carnevale points out that some Italian Americans found a way to use their knowledge of Italian in Office of Strategic Services (OSS) military teams intended for operations behind enemy lines. See Carnevale, 4, 16–18. Italian Americans volunteered for such military service in part as a demonstration of American loyalty, but undoubtedly also in part from a desire to see Italy freed from its Fascist grip. The Italian-American response to this “opportunity” as Carnevale terms it, is not unlike the likely impassioned response of the soldiers of the 99th Battalion to the request for volunteers for OSS teams to operate behind enemy lines in Norway. See Doug Bekke, “Norwegian-Americans and the 99th Infantry Battalion (Separate),” Military Historical Society of Minnesota [cited April 13, 2020]. Online: www.mnmilitarymuseum.org/files/5613/2261/5287/99th_Infantry_Battalion_Sep.pdf.
78. The 99th Battalion saw combat in France, the Ardennes, and Germany, before eventually shipping to Norway after the German surrender. *Washington Posten* made many references to the battalion from 1942 to 1945 in language suggesting an expectation that the readership was familiar with the 99th, and in want of updates. See “Amerikas Norsk-Talende Bataljon Er En Opmuntring,” *Washington Posten,* Nov. 20, 1942, 2; “Norsktalende Faar Inntre I Amerikas ‘Norske Bataljon,’” *Washington Posten,* Nov. 27, 1942, 1; “Alle Norsktalende Soldater Kan Söke Optakelse I 99. Infantri Battaljon,” *Washington Posten,* Dec. 11, 1942, 1; “Da Pres. Roosevelt Besökte Sine Norske Krigere,” *Washington Posten,* June 4, 1943, 1; “De Allierte Tropper I Norge Vil Bli Trukket Tilbake För Året Er Omme,” *Washington Posten,* June 8, 1945, 1; and “Norsk-Amerikansk Bataljon Omfattes Med Stor Interesse,” *Washington Posten,* June 15, 1945, 1.

79. "From Stjernen No. 7 Astoria, Oregon," *Dötre av Norge Paa Stillehavskysten* 6:5 (May 1942): 1.
80. "Niende April Ble En Stor Dag I Seattle," *Washington Posten,* April 16, 1943, 6. "Ninth of April Rally," and "Stor Norsk Fylking," ads, *Washington Posten,* April 9, 1943, 6.
81. 17th of May Program, Masonic Temple, Seattle, May 17, 1942; and May 16, 1943, in August Werner Papers, Special Collections, University of Washington Libraries.
82. "Klæs-Innsamlingen For Norges-Hjelpen," *Dötre av Norge Paa Stillehavskysten* 6:11 (November 1942): 2.
83. "Töi Samlet For Norges-Hjelpen Skal Nu Sendes," *Dötre av Norge Paa Stillehavskysten* 7:2 (February 1943): 2.
84. While Nancy Carnevale finds that the war hastened the demise of the Italian language in the Italian-American community, the same cannot be said regarding the use of the Norwegian language in the Norwegian-American communities of the Pacific Northwest. See Carnevale, 26.
85. "Greetings from the G. L. President," *Dötre av Norge Paa Stillehavskysten* 7:3 (March 1943): 1; "Storlosjepresidentens Rapport," *Dötre av Norge Paa Stillehavskysten* 8:6 (June 1944): 1.
86. "Referat Fra Storlosjen Dötre Av Norges 24. Storlosjemöte I Spokane, Wash., 8., 9. og 10. Juni 1944," *Dötre av Norge Paa Stillehavskysten* 8:7 (July 1944): 1–3.
87. "17 Mai I Seattle Feiret I Fullt Masonic Temple," *Washington Posten,* May 21, 1943, 6.
88. "Seattles 17 Mai Fest Ble Preget Av Werners Tale!," *Washington Posten,* May 25, 1945, 1. "Prof. Aug. Werner Taler Ved Seattles 17 Mai-Fest," *Washington Posten,* May 11, 1945, 6.
89. Elliott R. Barkan, "Race, Religion, and Nationality in American Society: A Model of Ethnicity—From Contact to Assimilation," *Journal of American Ethnic History* 14:2 (Winter 1995): 55–57.

Dressing Up in Postwar America

DREAMS, EXPERIENCES, AND EMBODIMENT AMONG FEMALE NORWEGIAN MIGRANTS IN NEW YORK, 1945–1955

Siv Ringdal

After living two years in Brooklyn, Jenny went back to her hometown in Norway for a visit. The young woman who returned to Norway had a different look than the girl who had left in 1947. She had a new hairdo, her clothes were in a different style, and she wore high-heeled, peep-toe sandals. Jenny can still recall her grandmother's reaction to her new American shoes: It was sinful to wear this kind of shoes! Her uncle, on the other hand, thought they could be of use. He joked about how she could wear them in the fields the next spring, helping him make small holes in the ground when he was planting his peas.[1]

Jenny Solaas[2] was sixteen years old when she left the peninsula of Lista on the southern coast of Norway for America. The story about her visit to Norway a couple of years later is amusing, but it also serves as a demonstration of the core argument of this article. The two years she had lived and worked in Brooklyn had an impact on Jenny in many ways. She had become familiar with the English language and the American job market; she had become acquainted with new kinds of food and leisure activities. However, life in America had also materialized itself on Jenny's body. Her clothes and shoes were in different colors and designs and her hair was styled in a new fashion. In a similar manner, the two years in New York had also affected Jenny's habits and body language. She had started to smoke, and high heels demanded a different way of walking than the flat shoes she had worn before she left Norway. Her new appearance provoked her grandmother and amused her uncle, and in this way brought some of the core values of her rural home town to the surface, such as obeying religious norms, and being strong and able to work rather than good looking. Jenny's new looks challenged these values.

Figure 1. Jenny photographed in a photography studio in Brooklyn not long after her arrival in America. The photograph was sent home to a good girlfriend in Norway. Courtesy of Jenny Hansen.

In this article, I aim to shed light on the crucial role that body and materiality plays in migration. I will examine this topic through the experiences of a group of young, unmarried women who migrated from the two counties of West and East Agder in the southernmost part of Norway to New York City in the ten years following the Second World War.[3] Upon their arrival in America, the young women's bodies became important tools for dealing with, negotiating, and adapting to their new everyday lives. In this article I will show how the young women used their bodies and the material culture of their surroundings as tools of negotiation—between traditional and modern female ideals, between a conservative religious and a more secular way of life, and between the culture of austerity in postwar Norway and the blossoming consumer culture in postwar New York. I will also demonstrate how the young women's experiences growing up during the Second World

War shaped their dreams and expectations in the postwar period. This had an impact on how they encountered, lived, and interpreted their new lives in America.

The bodily and material perspectives presented here were first introduced in my PhD dissertation in cultural history, which later formed the basis of my book *På høye hæler i Amerika* (On high heels in America), published in 2018.[4] The most important source material, in both the thesis and book, was qualitative interviews with some of the women who left their hometowns and villages in Agder and went to New York City in the two decades following the Second World War. Some of them left their homes permanently, while others returned to Norway after living for some years in the United States.[5] Other source material includes photographs, newspaper and magazine articles, and material culture.[6] This article stems from this previous research and is based on the interviews with the women who left Norway in the first ten years following the end of the Second World War, as well as supplemental source material, including magazine articles and photographs.

Before we can join the young postwar women on their journey to America, it is necessary to establish a few theoretical arguments and some contextualizing details. Therefore, I will start by presenting a few arguments about the importance of bodily and material aspects of migration. Then, I will give a brief presentation of the Agder counties and this region's transatlantic history. Jenny's story will be a continuous thread throughout the article. We will follow her from Norway to the United States and focus on her bodily and material experiences to illuminate her new life in America. I will refer to other women's experiences and memories too, trying to establish the universe of actions and practices in which this generation of female migrants formed a part.

The Materiality of Migration

As mentioned, I want to approach the young Agder women's migrant experiences with a focus on body and materiality. As a Norwegian cultural historian, I stand in a scholarly tradition where the study of material culture has been essential.[7] Generations of scholars before me have studied material culture, such as local building techniques, tools, folk dress, food, and more. The goal of these studies has been to analyze local adaptations and everyday life practices of the past.[8] In this text, I want to transfer the focus on material culture to the field of migration. Material culture has not been a prioritized field in historical studies of migration between Norway and America.[9] This is a paradox, since migration is, in so many ways, a material experience. In the introduction of a thematic volume of the journal *Mobilities,* the anthropologists Paul Basu and Simon Coleman express the relation between migration and materiality in the following way:

> To talk of migration and materiality gives only part of the picture that we wish to present; rather, we might just as easily say migration through materiality, since the one is impossible without the multi-dimensional yet vital presence of the other.[10]

Basu and Coleman argue that it is impossible to talk about migration without talking about materiality. Migration happens through materiality, and by relating to different kinds of materiality. Migration is a material experience. Just imagine the crossing of the Atlantic Ocean on a passenger ship. These vessels did not merely transport people from one destination to the other; they also shaped the travelers who were onboard. Material factors such as the size of the cabins and the division between first class and tourist class had an impact on how the passengers acted, moved, and how they related to each other. Moreover, aspects such as the smells from the kitchen located in the ship's tourist class, the steepness of the stairs between the floors, and the way the dining room was organized affected the passengers in certain ways. In the same manner, materiality played an important part in how the migrant encountered the new country. A new infrastructure, other ways of dressing, a different climate, and much more influenced how the newly arrived migrants acted and oriented themselves upon arrival. Through material culture, cultural and social similarities and differences are practiced and manifested. Therefore, material culture can provide an opening to understanding the cultural, social, and economic transformation processes of the migration experience and how migrants maneuver and negotiate being part of this process.

Embodying the Space of America

In this article, I will also show the importance of bringing the body into studies of historic migration. The body is of course partly material, and I will not go into a flesh-and-mind-discussion here. I rather want to emphasize the body's importance in the migration process. Migration means movement, and when migrants enter new and unfamiliar space, these spaces are experienced and interpreted with and through the body. Anthropologist Setha M. Low has introduced the phrase "embodied space." She defines it as "[the] location where human experience and consciousness take on material and spatial form."[11] I find Low's expression useful, because it shows how body and materiality both play an important role when we move between different spaces and communities. Entering new and unfamiliar space requires the gathering of information about the norms and practices inscribed in this particular space. In dialogue with the new space, the body transforms the new knowledge into bodily action.

Taking materiality, body, and space into account is also fruitful when analyzing (migrant) gender. Ethnologist Tine Damsholt argues that "it is precisely within this material-discursive concreteness—including the bodily and spatial concreteness—that gender occurs, or is 'done.'"[12] These perspectives have the advantage of shedding light on other aspects of the migrant experience than a more traditional approach does, and are well-suited when studying this particular group of women migrants from Agder. In this article about young migrant women leaving their homes in Norway and entering the metropolis of New York, this analytical approach can illuminate how these women moved between different spaces, both between their homes in Norway and New York and between different kinds of spaces within these two geographical areas. These spaces contained different resources and material expressions and had different norms and expectations. Inscribed in the young women's new workplaces, in the streets of Brooklyn, in church, in the shopping mall and the dance hall, were certain sociocultural expectations regarding how to look and act. These expectations could be related to a variety of cultural factors, such as how to act as an American (or a Norwegian American), how to act modern, how to behave as a consumer, as a good employee, a decent girl, and so on. So, how did these young women maneuver between different spaces with their diverse expectations? Moreover, in what ways did the war have an impact on how the young girls related to these spaces, norms, and ideals?

Agder and America

When Jenny left Agder in February 1947, it had been one-and-a-half years since the Second World War had ended. The Nazi capitulation marked the starting point of a new era in Norway. In valleys and villages, in larger towns and cities, a new life emerged in peacetime. Local governments had to re-form, houses and infrastructure had to be rebuilt, and new industries and jobs were created.[13] As the borders opened, the end of the war also led to people moving in new ways and directions. In West and East Agder, the inhabitants quickly reestablished a local pattern of movement that had been maintained since the nineteenth century. They traveled to America to live and work. Although many of them settled in the United States permanently, most of them intended only to spend some years in America before returning home to Norway.[14]

Located in the southernmost region of Norway, the Agder region consists of a long coastal line from the town of Risør in the east to the town of Flekkefjord in the west.[15] Norway's southernmost point, the peninsula of Lindesnes, is also in Agder. The coastal line is dotted with villages and small towns, almost like pearls on a necklace, and the natural landscape comprises archipelagoes and beaches, as well as a rougher landscape in the west. The Agder region also has a large inland area, containing valleys and mountains. The best-known valley is the Setesdal, where traditional ways of dressing, farming, and living were kept alive until the early twentieth century.[16] While farming, forestry, and in some areas, mining were the most important ways of earning a living in the inlands, the coastal population depended heavily on the bounty of the sea. In the rural areas, most of the population had small farms, but the farms only contributed to a small part of the household income. Consequently, the population combined small-scale farming with more profitable industries.[17] Many men worked in the fisheries, both locally and farther north along the Norwegian coast.[18] Several women also had seasonal income from sea-related industries, like processing fish or gathering seagrass both for use as animal fodder and for use in the iodine industries.[19] A large part of the male population also worked as sailors, both on vessels carrying goods and on vessels carrying people along the Norwegian coast, as well as in the international shipping transportation industry. Most of the sailors worked on vessels owned by local shipowners.[20]

Although there had been some early migration from Agder in the first half of the nineteenth century, migration from the region accelerated in the last few decades of the nineteenth century. It was a migration closely connected with the maritime sector, and often timed in reaction to crises in both the fishing and shipping industries. The fisheries failed several years in a row and the local sail vessels lost the competition of tonnage and freight to larger international steamships. Young men who had been employed in these two sectors began to emigrate to America, especially to the East Coast, where they took work on American ships. Many eventually went ashore and started a new life in America.

After a while, other inhabitants from Agder, with no ties to the maritime sector, followed the sailor's movements. From the 1890s and up to the mid-1960s the two counties had the highest level of overseas migrants per capita in Norway.[21] In Jenny's home town of Lista, for instance, one-fourth of the population worked or had been working in America in 1910, and in 1920 this had increased to one-third of the population.[22] A characteristic part of the migration from Agder is that the migrants brought a seamen's mentality along with them. They regarded their trip to the United States as temporary—like a seaman who boarded a vessel—and their plan was eventually to return with money in the bank and a brighter future back home in Norway.[23] Although many ended up in America on a permanent basis, their original plan was often to go back.

A large part of the Agder migrants settled in Brooklyn, New York. A Norwegian community had been established there in the late nineteenth century, due to its close proximity to the maritime sector.[24] Consequently, the community was located near the Brooklyn harbor in Red Hook. As the community grew, and new groups from other industries came along, the community extended farther northeast to the Carroll Gardens district. Here, the crime rate was lower and the surroundings nicer for Norwegian-American families. As other national and ethnic groups settled in the neighborhood and new parts of Brooklyn were developed, the Norwegian community gradually relocated farther south. By the 1930s the Norwegian community in Brooklyn, New York, had its center in the Sunset Park and Bay Ridge area in the southern part of the borough. In 1940, New York City had fifty-four thousand first- and second-generation Norwegians, most of them living in this area.[25]

Everyday Life during the Nazi Occupation

Jenny was nearly ten years old when war broke out in Norway and almost fifteen when it ended.[26] The war was part of her life in these formative years, a time span in which she left childhood and entered youth and early adulthood. Jenny was born in Brooklyn, a daughter of two Norwegian immigrants. She came to Norway as a small child, first to her father's hometown of Mosterhamn on the west coast of Norway. Then they moved to her mother's home town of Lista in the western part of Agder, when Jenny was eight. When the Nazis occupied Norway, Jenny's father was back in America, running a deli on Fifth Avenue near Sunset Park, Brooklyn. For almost five years they had no contact, and Jenny's mother had a tough time, running a household with five children on not much income. Luckily, Jenny's grandparents lived close by, and could lend the family a hand.

For the local population of Agder, the Nazi occupation had a large impact on many levels. Some lost their loved ones when British planes attacked strategic German targets, though these were rare incidents. Others participated in the illegal resistance movement. Some were caught and became prisoners of war, either in Norway or in Nazi Germany. Most inhabitants of Agder were not affected in this violent and dramatic way, but their lives were still considerably influenced. The occupying power introduced a new set of rules, and the locals had the daily fear of the consequences if they chose to break them. A large part of the Agder population had relatives and friends overseas, either on Norwegian ships in the Atlantic or living in America. The occupiers forbade the use of radios, and all personal communication was eventually cut off.[27] When they did not have any contact, many had to cope with worries about how their loved ones were doing. The war did not just affect the population emotionally. It also had a huge impact on people's daily lives. Some

Figure 2. Jenny photographed with her mother and siblings in Lista in the 1930s. Courtesy of Jenny Hansen.

had to vacate their homes to provide housing for Nazi officers and soldiers. Others lived too close to strategic Allied bombing targets and had to move to safer areas.[28]

The war also led to the lack of many different resources that people depended on in their daily lives. One product after the other disappeared from the market, and in the last two years of the war, the German occupiers introduced rationing on nearly all food products.[29] Textiles, fuel, and other products and essentials were also rationed. By the time the war ended, many had not tasted sugar and coffee in years, and they had wardrobes marked by long-time use and the lack of textiles.

When the British bombing escalated, Jenny's family had to move out of their home. Jenny recalled that her mother was in despair. She remembered her mother saying, "I have five kids and a bicycle. Where am I going to go?"[30] Their resources were also limited. The rationing cards were restricted, and the quality of the food worsened as the war went on. While other families in Lista lived on farms and had better access to produce, Jenny's family did not have the same supply of food. Her grandparents had a fruit garden, so they were able to obtain some extra vitamins in their diet during certain parts of the year. However, Jenny was thin, and her mom worried. The bread was of poor quality, which led to frustration, but also to a good deal of humor. Jenny recalled that they used to joke about the bread, saying things like, "Well, you know, the bread we ate. That was the old couch, we just ground it up." The bad bread also led to flatulence, and consequently a common expression during the war was, "Have you heard the new bread?"[31] After Jenny's confirmation at age fifteen, her mother sent her to the nearest town of Farsund, where she got job as a housekeeper in a well-situated family. In this way, Jenny's mom secured her daughter access to a better diet.

Up-to-Date with the Wrong Side Out

Despite the scarce resources available, Jenny recalls how she and her girlfriends wanted to dress fashionably. However, in the wartime universe, up-to-date dressing meant the creative use of what was at hand. When Jenny confirmed her vows to God in front of her minister in the fall of 1944, she was part of the last batch of youths to be confirmed in the parish during the Nazi occupation.[32] Jenny remembers the day well. She felt so grown up! She had her first permanent hairdo done, wore a dress and a hat, a woolen coat, and new gloves. The hat had originally been her grandfather's, but she got it before her confirmation and had it remade in a feminine style. The gloves were made of fish skin, a material quite common for gloves and shoes due to the lack of leather fabrics. Her mother had bought a piece of fabric with a ration card, and she sewed the dress for Jenny. Before the war, the local costume tradition for girls when getting confirmed was to have two dresses. They would usually have one for *overhøringsdagen* [questioning day]. This was the day they would answer the minister's questions in front of the congregation and show their knowledge of the Bible and the results of their preparations. They would also have a long white dress for *golvsøndagen* [floor-Sunday], the most ceremonious day, when they would stand in front of the altar and the minister would bless them and lay his hand on their heads. During the war years, this was too demanding a practice. The white dress was abolished, and the girls used the same dress both days, as Jenny did.

The lack of textiles led to creative solutions and maximum use of what was available. People went on using their clothes, and patched and mended them. When the coats, pants, and dresses were thoroughly worn, industrious hands would split up the seams and transform the different pieces of fabric into new garments. If a surface was too marked by long-time use, the fabric would be turned inside out so the new garment would look less threadbare. Jenny remembers an episode where her mother had been to town to buy fabric for a new coat. She could not understand why Jenny was so interested in the reverse side. "That's because I want to see how it is going to look when I get it," Jenny replied. This way of thinking also continued in the years following the end of the war. Textile rationing continued for six years after 1945, and it took more years before the strict restrictions on the import of foreign textiles and fabrics ended.[33]

Dreams and Desire in Norwegian Mass Media following the War

"Amerikanerinnen klær seg ungt" (American women dress up young) was one of the headlines on the front cover of the popular Norwegian women's magazine *Alle Kvinners Blad* in the late fall of 1945.[34] The headline was in great contrast to the cover photo on the same issue, picturing an elderly woman dressed up in a traditional folk dress from the valley of Hallingdal. When the readers opened this brand-new issue in their homes, just a few months after the Second World War had ended, they could look at stunning photos of American models dressed in the latest fashion. The photos were black and white, but the captions described the colors and materials of the different garments and the bold color combinations in detail. The captions and text of the article described how the modern American woman was both sporty and elegant. The fashion in America that fall demanded a slim figure, and the style was youthful and refined. The text also referred to an expression, supposedly American, saying "In America grandmothers dress like *backfisches* [synonymous with flapper], in Europe the *backfisches* dress like grandmothers."[35]

The same issue also had an article about how the women in the mountain area of Randen in Hallingdal got hold of seventy-four parachutes in beautiful, thick yellow silk, that were used when the Allied Americans dropped containers

Figure 3. Cover of the popular women's magazine *Alle Kvinners Blad,* from November 1945. The elderly woman featured on the magazine's cover is dressed in the traditional folk dress from Hallingdal.

Figure 4. In the magazine article "Amerikanerinnen klær seg ungt" from 1945, American women and their latest fashions are described. According to the article, American women's dress was both sporty and elegant, their style was youthful and refined, but it demanded a slim figure. Interior spread of *Alle Kvinners Blad,* November 1945.

Amerikanerinnen klær seg ungt

«I Amerika kler bestemødrene seg som backfischer, i Europa backfischene som bestemødre.» Slik setter amerikanerne tingen på spissen når de skal definere forskjellen på amerikansk og europèisk mote. Vi kan jo også si det slik at amerikanerinnen i alle aldrer kler seg ungt. At denne ungdommelige moten er både praktisk og flatterende, det vet vi jo, ettersom amerikanske damer hører til de mest velkledde som fins.

En annen grunn til å kike amerikanerinnens garderobe litt nærmere etter i sømmene er at hun, stort sett, kler seg akkurat så uvørent, sporty og likevel kvinnelig flatterende, som vi liker. Derfor betenker vi oss ikke på å kopiere klærne hennes og stjele idéer når vi kan komme over dem.

Skal vi i få ord slå fast hva som er det karakteristiske ved høstens linjer på den andre siden av dammen, så fester vi oss først ved skjørtevidden. Noe tilbakeslag mot de vide skjørtene som nå har dominert motebildet i 6—8 år, later ikke til å være på trappene. Og det skal vi bare være takknemlige for — det er en både praktisk og ungdommelig mote. Den aksentuerte hoftevidden som Paris går inn for, er øyensynlig ikke særlig aktuell for amerikanerinnen. Derimot er det en detalj som går igjen på en rekke amerikanske modeller. De trekvartlange ermene — enten de nå syes trekvartlange eller man simpelthen — med tilfeldighetens preg — hipser opp de lange ermene så de bare rekker litt nedenfor albuene.

with guns, ammunition, and other military material near the end of the war.[36] The article does not say anything about how the silk was used, but it is likely that many girls and women in Hallingdal wore garments in yellow silk in 1945 and the following years, not merely the traditional folk dress like the one featured on the magazine's cover.

These two magazine articles are examples of how America was presented in the mainstream Norwegian mass media following the end of the Second World War. America was the successful, handsome war ally who had led Norway to the happy outcome of peace. When the war ended, these warm feelings of friendship mixed with a variety of input coming from across the Atlantic Ocean, such as film, music, the introduction of new brands and products, and the implementation of an American cultural policy (the Marshall Plan).[37] The end of the war led to an era of new dreams and desires. People longed for new products and goods, for material growth and prosperity. In this process of establishing a new and modern life, America was of great inspiration. This was not a new phenomenon; Norwegians had also been inspired and influenced by America in the 1920s and 1930s, with Hollywood films, jazz, and the introduction of new fashion and products.[38] In postwar Norway, Norwegians again looked to America, both on a personal and on a more public level. America, Americans, and American products became objects of admiration, and America the symbol of a new, modern postwar lifestyle.

In the years following the war, Norwegian newspapers and magazines had many advertisements for American products, such as Coca Cola, Kellogg's, Lux soap, and Veet hair removal products, just to mention a few. The advertisements were often very explicit about the products' American origin. Other products might not have been of American origin, but the brand owners wanted the readers to associate the products with America anyhow. For instance, an ad for the latex paint Splendex claimed that it was of "American type," despite the fact that it was produced in Oslo by a Norwegian manufacturing company. The skyscraper featured in the ad helped underscore the association between the brand and America. Another ad in the same magazine, for the suspender Comfy Roll-On, also mentions that the elastics are of the "American type."[39] The advertising bureaus'

Figure 5. An ad for Splendex paint in *Alle Kvinners Blad,* November 1945. Although a Norwegian manufacturer in Oslo produced the paint, the ad claims that it is of an "American type," and features an image of a skyscraper. The name of the paint also refers to the English word "splendid."

efforts to associate the products with America seems to have been to make the goods more appealing to the consumers.

Especially the young generation dreamed of America in the years following the war. Many young girls would have scrapbooks with American movie stars and musicians. They would cut out pictures of models in the latest American fashions and try to copy the garments, and they would go to the movies and watch Hollywood films.[40] However, the young generation's admiration of America also had its critics. In a radio broadcast, the writer Sigurd Evensmo complained about the new "ok generation" (*okei-generasjonen*), who wore jeans from Texas and "went rocking" into their future on their noisy motorcycles.[41]

Transatlantic Relations in Agder

On the southern coast of Norway, the feelings toward America were similarly positive, although, because of the large previous migration to America, they blended with American impulses of a more local kind. In Agder, the population had its own American cultural entrepreneurs in addition to the more mainstream U.S. contributions provided in the mass media.

For over half a century, a steady stream of Agder migrants had returned home after months, years, or decades living in the United States. They influenced and inspired their family and friends back home with American fashion and goods, new ideas and ideals, and a more American mindset.[42] A common migration pattern in the area was that young adults left their homes in Agder for a new life in America, with the majority ending up in Brooklyn, New York. Many met their future husband or wife there, usually not American, but from towns and villages back home. Most of the young women who migrated took work as maids, the men as carpenters or in the maritime sector. They fell in love, married, and settled in the Norwegian community in Brooklyn.[43] Many Agder migrants planned to return to Norway after some time in America. Although many ended up living there permanently, they had seldom considered their first crossing of the Atlantic as something definite. In this manner, the Agder migrants differed from the generations of Norwegian migrants leaving Norway during most of the nineteenth century. They have more in common with, for instance, Italian migrants living in other quarters of Brooklyn, who also often had the goal of an Atlantic passage back home to Europe.[44] Consequently, in many families in Agder, several generations had been in America to live and work. In some families, for instance, both grandfather, father, and son had worked as carpenters in New York.[45]

When the Agder couples in diaspora had children, and the children were close to school age, many felt they had to make a choice. Some decided to stay in America, others went back home to Norway with trunks and containers filled with all their belongings. Many also bought new American goods for their future in Norway, products that were not available in Agder at the time or were different from the same products back home. Several of the men, who had been working in the building industry, brought blueprints of suburban house types, and built an American house as their new home. After settling in Norway, the wife would take care of the children and the daily running of the household. Many times, the husbands would return to New York for work, especially men who worked in construction and carpentry. A common migration pattern would be that these men left home around Easter and returned to Norway before Christmas. However, it was expensive to go home, and they could not return every year. Consequently, a common expression among the children in areas where this kind of commuting was widespread was, “My dad is coming home in one Christmas” or “My dad is coming home in two Christmases.”[46]

Because of this local migration pattern, several generations of Agder children grew up hearing of, relating to, and longing for America. They heard stories about their mothers working as maids in upper-class households in Manhattan in the early twentieth century, or their fathers working on building the Chrysler Building and other projects in New York. They would receive letters and gifts from family members, maybe a doll or a puzzle, and a package of Life Savers. One man, born in 1918, grew up with his father away for years. He remembers how he learned the names of all the bridges crossing the East River between Manhattan and Brooklyn. When he later went to New York as a young man, he described his encounter “as if you came to something familiar, although you had never been there before.” He arrived in New York on a maritime vessel, and the ship passed the Statue of Liberty. Then he could see the skyline. “It was as if I came to something very familiar. I knew this city, although I had never been there. So it was part of our lives growing up.”[47]

“America Parcels” with Dresses and Coffee

When the Second World War ended, the local communities in Agder resumed their transatlantic relations. News and letters from America arrived, and most of the households received “America parcels” (*amerikapakker*) as well. These parcels brought awaited goods, foods, and textiles to a population craving all sorts of products after five years of regulations and scarcity. With their smells and textures, the America parcels were a tactile materialization of the wealth and material prosperity of America, which nourished the dreams of the generation growing up. Jenny remembers the thrill and excitement when they got their first America parcel after the war had ended. She recalls her mother saying, “I need to put the kettle on straight away! I don’t know how many people have asked me if it contains coffee.

And I can smell that there's coffee in it!" Her mother would get a note from the post office when a parcel had arrived, and the entire family all gathered around the big box in the living room.[48]

Most of the parcels came from relatives and friends in America, but some also received packages from unknown Norwegian Americans or Norwegian-American organizations who wanted to help. The America parcels were boxes and cases in different sizes containing a variety of items. In the Norwegian-American community in Brooklyn, the inhabitants could buy ready-made boxes of different sizes, containing diverse combinations of foods and products, to send home. Others made their own parcels, and they would fill them with many different items. Common items to put in would be used clothes and different kinds of food, such as coffee, sugar, pasta, canned and fresh fruit, chocolate, and chewing gum. They could also contain household items such as soap and detergent, kitchen appliances, towels and bedlinens, to mention a few examples.[49]

Many young Agder girls were most excited about the clothes in the America parcels. In contrast to the worn-out clothes in use in Norway after the war, the secondhand American garments seemed like new. Many recalled them as being brighter in color, and of other materials than they were used to. At the end of the Second World War, the American production of synthetic fibers, such as nylon, could resume. During the war years, this production was directed toward the military industry, for making parachutes, among other uses.[50] Now the magical fiber nylon again could be transformed into shirts and dresses in bright, fashionable colors.[51] Most of the inhabitants in Agder were unfamiliar with synthetic fabrics when they first came in the mail from relatives and friends in America.

Jenny remembers that one of the America parcels contained clothes she could wear for her first Christmas in peacetime, consisting of a beautiful dress, nylon stockings, and a nice pair of shoes. The garments stood in great contrast to the clothes Jenny wore the last years of the war. "The clothes back home were gray, sad, and dark, because they were usually made from garments my mother had gotten from some elderly people," she explains.[52] Her mother would split the seams and make clothing for Jenny and her siblings. With new—although used—garments from America, Jenny and her girlfriends felt "like a million dollars."

The end of the war also led many people to return to Agder to see their families and friends. These Norwegian Americans arrived home, many in modern, stylish clothes, and some with different habits and manners. Many people in Agder remember them vividly. They stood out from the local crowd with their modern suits, pearl-rimmed glasses, and colorful dresses. Some recalled the Norwegian Americans' white teeth, others their self-assured body language and their English words and phrases.[53] A woman born in 1929 remembered one of the first celebrations of the Norwegian Constitution Day after the war. Two young Norwegian-American girls participated in the parade, and they stood out with their petticoats and tulle dresses, almost looking like angels, she recalled.[54] Jenny remembered one of her mother's friends visiting from Brooklyn a short time after the war. She was not beautiful, more average looking, but she made a great impression on Jenny and her cousin with her nice clothes, a beautifully veiled hat, and her hair perfectly arranged at the nape of her neck.[55]

The Norwegian-American women were of great inspiration to the young girls growing up on the southern tip of Norway. The local teenagers admired American actors and other popular icons. However, they also had their local American stars, cultural agents who made a strong impression on the generations growing up, and who represented a more attainable dream they could follow. These Norwegian Americans were also the ones who ensured that the traditional commuting between Agder and the United States was kept up after the war. They would take on the risk of giving the younger generations who wanted to emigrate the necessary financial guarantee, and they would assist their Norwegian relatives and neighbors upon their arrival in New York, helping them get their first job and their first home in America.[56]

In an Old Coat with Paper Whirling in the Streets

Jenny arrived in Manhattan on Valentine's Day in 1947. She did not know any English, except for "yes," "no," and "I love you." Her mother had traveled to America the year before, to reunite with Jenny's father in Brooklyn. Jenny's siblings also emigrated in the following years. Jenny's first impression of America was disappointing. There had been a heavy snowfall, but the snow was all gray, colored by

Figure 6. Fifth Avenue in Brooklyn, photographed from Fifty-Second Street and Northeast in the late 1950s. Along with Eighth Avenue, these two avenues were the most important streets in the Norwegian-American community in Brooklyn in the postwar era. Norwegian shops, cafes, and organizations were located there, and in the photograph it is possible to see a glimpse of one of these businesses, Nilsen's Jewelers, on the right side. Photograph courtesy of Ernst Nodeland.

the ashes from heavy coal heating the city. "Just wait until you come to Bay Ridge," Jenny's aunt said after she and Jenny's mother had picked her up on Pier 8, East River. Nevertheless, even there, it was not as she imagined. Because of the snowfall, the garbage trucks could not empty the garbage bins all over the city. They were overfilled and paper whirled around in the windy streets.[57]

On one of her first days, her aunt gave Jenny a challenge. She thought it was best to expose her niece to new situations. Her aunt considered it an effective way to learn both the language and culture. Jenny remembered an episode where her lack of competence became visible. Her aunt gave her the following task:

> "I want you to go to the grocery store. There you'll buy five oranges and four apples and put them in a bag. Just help yourself in the store," she said, and then she gave me money. When I had done what she had requested, I didn't know how to say,

> "How much do I owe you?" So I just said "money." And then I went back to Aunt Magda and said, "They were very busy, talking about a banana boat. But Aunt Magda, what is a 'greenhorn'?" She answered, "Jenny, just don't mind. They were talking about you." Because what they said was, "she's a greenhorn right off the banana boat."[58]

Long before Jenny had opened her mouth to say the word "money," the shop assistants understood that she was a newcomer. She did not just lack the right words and expressions; her clothing also revealed her new arrival from the Old World. Jenny was still wearing the woolen coat she got for her confirmation day, and it probably had an unfashionable look. As a newcomer, Jenny had not learned how to move or act in the new space she had become part of, the urban landscape. For instance, she had never been to a self-service shop before. Back home in Norway they would buy groceries from shopkeepers standing behind counters, and the first self-service store on Lista was not established until 1962. Jenny did not know all the procedures in this unfamiliar kind of shop, a lack of competence that probably was quite visible for the people working there. They regarded Jenny as a "greenhorn," a newcomer that still had the appearance and behavior of the Old World. Although her old woolen coat was useful those winter days in her new American life, she felt clumsy, insecure, and out of place.

Embodying Work

Jenny's aunt ran a hiring agency in Brooklyn, aiding newly arrived women, especially Norwegians, in finding suitable work. She found Jenny a housekeeping job in a Syrian-American family, taking care of three children. Jenny liked the job. The family was nice, and the lady of the house took good care of her new employee. Jenny remembered how she taught her English. "She was very nice. She used to point at things in the house and say 'this is . . .' So, I picked up the language fast," she recalled.[59] Most of the girls did not know much English upon their arrival, and in this way, domestic work was an arena where the young women expanded their vocabulary through being exposed to new tasks and items and to new and unfamiliar situations. Domestic jobs were also a place where the young women gradually became familiar with other aspects of American culture, like the multiethnic America with its different religions, foods, and traditions, but also with its class structure, and a white, old stock ideal permeating nearly all aspects of society. Some also became familiar with the American standards of feminine beauty in their workplace, with their female employer advising them on how to dress, do their hair, shave body hair, walk on high heels, and more.

Nearly all the young Agder women started their working career in America doing housework and taking care of the children of middle- and upper-class families in New York. They followed in their mothers', and some even in their grandmothers', footsteps. The work could be tiresome and hard. Because of their newcomer status and limited knowledge of American society and language, they were easy to exploit. Some were underpaid and had employers who gave them unacceptable working conditions or tasks. One woman, Kari Gaupeland,[60] told me how she had to take down the chandelier every week, dismantle it, and brush all the small prisms it consisted of.[61] Some had employers who sexually assaulted them.[62] Others, like Jenny, had experiences that were of the more positive kind. With a good relation to their employers, their workplace became an arena where they could learn about different aspects of American culture. In these jobs the employers often took on the responsibility as mentors who wanted to give their employees a better start in their new land.

Kari, the woman who had to clean the chandelier every week, eventually quit and got a new job. She remembered the good relationship she had with her new employers. She ate her meals together with them, they went out for dinners and trips, they bought her gifts and arranged her birthday party. When she was having problems with the moist heat in the warm summer days, they bought her salt tablets and other remedies and put a fan in her room. Her female employer gave her hair a new style, bought her nice dresses, and advised her about American routines of feminine beauty and hygiene. It was even her male employer, who worked as a doctor, who persuaded her to wear high heels:

And the doctor told me, because I never wore high heels because I was so tall. So, I had to go through the hall when I was going out on a Saturday night for dance and he called me in, and he said: "Are you ever going to wear high heels?" "But Doctor Carrougher, I am so tall" [I said]. He said: "But that's the beauty of it." So, from then on I went out and bought high heels and I wore nothing but heels after that.[63]

However, in contrast to the generations of Agder women before them, the postwar generation of migrant women did not necessarily stay in these jobs for long. They were part of a more individualistic generation seeking independence. Their mothers and the generation of migrants before them had worked as live-in housekeepers, doing domestic work until they got married. They had their Thursdays and Sundays off, while returning to their rooms in their employer's house by night. The postwar generation wanted to have less supervised spare time. Consequently, after they had learned enough English, they left their domestic jobs, rented a flat with girlfriends from home, and took jobs in stores, dressmaker shops, offices, and factories. In 1950s Brooklyn, many Agder women worked for Beech Nut, packing chewing gum on the assembly line. Others served in the Norwegian-American restaurants in Brooklyn, or sorted screws at Schreider's factory.[64]

The Consumer Landscape and the New Language of Dressing Up

In their leisure time, Jenny and the other young women from Agder would enter the consumer landscape of New York. At first, it was unknown territory; they had never been in large shopping malls before, with racks and racks filled with garments in a variety of colors and fashions. They had never taken an escalator before, and needed to learn how to maneuver the shops and act in fitting rooms and in front of counters. However, they learned fast, and going to the shopping malls and smaller boutiques in Brooklyn became a weekly activity, buying a new dress for the next dance, with shoes and sometimes a tote and gloves to match. The young Agder women embodied the consumer landscape of New York and dressed in the latest

Figure 7. A group of young Norwegian women photographed in Brooklyn in the mid-1950s. Photographer unknown. Courtesy of Per Ove Eikeland.

fashions. They became familiar with the American grammar of dressing up, which stood in great contrast to the practice they brought with them from home. In their childhood and youth during the war years and early postwar years in Agder, their clothes were, for the most part, sewed at home. As young girls, they had learned how to take care of and mend their clothes to make them last as long as possible. In New York, people followed fashion. Everyone could buy ready-made clothes, and there were fashionable clothes for both well-filled and slimmer wallets. The quality would differ, and the shoes and seams of the dress might just last for one evening at the dance hall. Nevertheless, one looked smart and up-to-date.[65]

Just as it demanded knowledge to sew one's own dress, the American way of consuming fashion required competence. The young women had to learn how to combine garments and accessories to make a complete but also culturally acceptable outfit. Agder women who had been in New York longer would teach the newcomers. If they needed correction they would try to advise. This was also the case when they tried out other products. Several of the girls had not used makeup before they came to America. It was expensive and in rural Agder not always easy to get hold of, and it was also something many considered both sinful and improper to wear. The young women in Brooklyn would try out the new products together, and they would correct each other if their looks became too exaggerated or indecent. Although American fashion and American ideals were of importance to the young Norwegian women, the response they got from their countrywomen and men in the Norwegian community were also of great importance.

The young women embraced American fashion, many buying a new dress every week. After years of material scarcity, it was a great joy to look up-to-date, and the petticoats and dresses filled up their closets and wardrobes. Some found it hard to get used to the American use and discard mentality. One woman explained how she came to Brooklyn in an American dress she had received in an America parcel. She thought the dress was so beautiful. However, when her aunt saw it, she asked her niece to put it straight in the garbage bin. Many solved this dilemma by sending their used dresses and coats to relatives back home. This way, they could be fashionable without having a bad conscience.[66]

Embodying the "Right-Kind-of-Girl" in Agder and America

I started this article with a story about Jenny's return to Norway after a couple of years in New York. The story showed how Jenny's new looks and manners provoked, and in this way, revealed some of the core values of her home culture. One central ideal was to be a good worker, which meant to have large work capacity, and to be able to do a variety of tasks, both in the right manner and in an efficient way. Jenny's fashionable look led her uncle to make fun of her. For him, Jenny's clothes and appearance probably materialized a culture and an ideal that focused more on looking good than being able to work well. Jenny's dress and peep-toe sandals were not suited for farm work. Her shoes represented an American feminine ideal that clashed with the traditional qualities women had been valued by in this community. Jenny's shoes, revealing her bare toes, also provoked her religious grandmother. They did not follow the norms of proper and modest dressing, and Jenny's bare toes could lead others to sinful thoughts and improper behavior. The feminine ideals in Agder and America were markedly different, and it required a different set of material and normative resources to embody them. The religious ideal of dressing and acting, which the young women had grown up with in Agder, stood in great contrast to the postwar American feminine ideal. How did the young women maneuver between these ideals?

A conservative religious belief dominated the Agder counties up to the mid-twentieth century. This conservative approach to Lutheran Christianity had a strong hold in both the State church and in the numerous prayer houses scattered all over Agder. Many practices and activities were regarded as sinful, like playing cards, listening to popular music, going to the movies, and much more.[67] This religious control was particularly strict toward youth, and especially strict concerning young women. Young women who grew up in religious families had to adjust their behavior and looks according to many norms and rules. For instance, they were not allowed to wear any makeup, bleach their hair, wear dresses showing too much décolletage or too-short skirts, smoke cigarettes, drink alcohol, and much more. Interestingly, even women growing up in less religious families also remembered that they sometimes had to relate to these religious rules. The religious norms might have offered a good way for parents to control their daughters' behavior, and might have also given these families a way to prevent local gossip about their young girls.[68]

The most problematic activity was dancing. If you professed being a Christian, dancing was a taboo. Thus, this activity split the youth culture in two. There were the more secular oriented youth who went to the dance halls and there were the conservative Christians who would not enter such a location under any circumstances. Dancing was so problematic that some of the most conservative Christians would not even enter a room where there had been dancing in the past, although it might have been months or even years since it took place. It was also often problematic to move between the dance hall and different kinds of religious spaces. For instance, you could not go to the dance hall on a Saturday night and then attend the Lord's Supper in church Sunday morning. The young ones growing up had embodied these rules; they knew how to maneuver between these different kinds of spaces. The conservative Christians performed their embodied choreography, while the more secular embodied a different one.[69]

Upon their arrival in America, the young women met other ways of practicing religious beliefs. The God they heard of in America seemed to be less strict and more forgiving than the God they knew from back home. In American congregations, the youth could dance, and the women wore lipstick. In general, Americans seemed less occupied with labeling activities and products as sinful. Many of the women who arrived in New York in the postwar years recalled the contrast between the strict and conservative way of life back home and the less strict and more open-minded way of life in America. One woman remembered how they used to say, "Put it under the table!" if there was a knock on the door while her family had a beer back home in Norway. In America they would rather say, "Would you like to have a drink?" if someone came.[70]

In many ways, the metropolis gave the young women a chance to make their own choices. They could free themselves from the strict rules and control, going out dancing, have a drink, smoke cigarettes, and wear lipstick. If they wanted to, they could also choose to live more conservatively. In the Norwegian community in Brooklyn, there were many Lutheran congregations, ranging from conservative to liberal.[71] Many of the young women chose to free themselves from the strict rules and regulations. They went to the dance hall as many as three times a week and seized the chance to live a freer life. Others explained that their church congregation represented the most important part of their lives in America. That was where all the social activities happened; their flats were merely a place to sleep. They never went to the dance hall, neither in Agder, nor in Brooklyn. Several underscored how they enjoyed being able to make their own choice, and to be able to commute between secular and religious spaces in new ways. In New York, they could go dancing in the dance hall on Saturday night, then go to church Sunday morning, attending service and catching up with people from home. Moreover, the active churchgoers could now go to the movies, or watch a show on Broadway, without fear of judgment.[72]

Jenny's Beauty Studio

Although Jenny's first impression of New York had not been the best, she gradually became familiar with the asphalt and buildings, the urban sounds and smells

Figure 8. Jenny was active in the Norwegian Folk Dance Society in Brooklyn. In the photo, Jenny and a young man from the Norway Ski Club are posing for Norwegian-American photographer Rudy Larsen. The photo was used in an ad for the 17th of May Festival, which was arranged at the Livingston Ball Room in May 1954. Photograph by Rudy Larsen. Courtesy of Jenny Hansen.

and her new American everyday life. Jenny discovered the Finn Hall, a dancing place in the Finnish quarter of Brooklyn, and she and her girlfriends went there dancing as often as they could. Jenny also became a member of Folkedanslaget, a Norwegian-American dancing group.[73] They performed in their Norwegian folk costumes, dancing traditional dances on a variety of occasions both within and outside the Norwegian-American community. The dance group was an important social arena for Jenny when she was a newcomer.

After some years working as a housekeeper, Jenny decided to become a hairdresser. In 1956 she opened Jenny's Beauty Studio on Fifth Avenue, in the same quarter where her parents ran a deli.[74] Jenny ran the salon for twelve years. It was a busy time, but Jenny enjoyed the job. Several of her customers were

Figure 9. Jenny in her salon, Jenny's Beauty Studio, on Fifth Avenue, not far from Sunset Park. In the photo, Jenny is doing the hair of Miss Norway 1960. Photograph by Rudy Larsen. Courtesy of Jenny Hansen.

Norwegian Americans, but Jenny also had many customers with backgrounds from other places. In this way, Jenny got to know the multifaceted national and ethnic mosaic of New York through her salon. Jenny recruited Norwegian-American women as trainees in her salon. When the winners of two beauty contests in the Norwegian-American neighborhood were named, it was Jenny who did their hair and got them ready for a photo shoot.[75] Jenny also advised her young customers. She remembered a young woman who came to the salon to do her hair and makeup before her wedding.[76] This young woman often overdid her makeup and her necklines, making her look cheap. Jenny toned down her looks and gave her a more subtle and modest appearance.[77]

Jenny also remembered how some of the conservative Christians brought their pietistic norms along to Brooklyn, and how these thoughts were practiced in some of the more conservative Norwegian-speaking congregations. She particularly remembered an episode where two women, belonging to the same congregation, came to her salon to do their hair. One of them was getting a permanent, while the other one was dyeing her hair. The woman having a permanent expressed her discontent with the woman dyeing her hair: "It's sinful to dye the hair. How can you do that? No, let me have the hair color God gave me," Jenny recalled her saying. Jenny disliked the condemnation of the other woman and said, "Well, she is just dyeing her hair back to the color God gave her. But God never gave you curls."[78]

Jenny also found the love of her life in Brooklyn in the 1950s. His name was Benny Hansen, and he was a sailor from Denmark. They married, and in the late 1960s, the couple moved out of Brooklyn and settled in Upstate New York. Jenny and Benny did not have children of their own, but Jenny had several siblings in America, and a large number of nieces and nephews. She also had close relatives in Norway, and in the early 2000s the couple decided to return to Europe. They settled in Jenny's home country and bought a house in the city of Kristiansand in Agder. Benny has passed away, but Jenny still lives there. Every year she returns to America to visit family and old friends from her years in Brooklyn—and to do some shopping.

Contrasting Worlds

For the young women migrating from Agder to New York in the years following the end of the Second World War, America meant a journey from material scarcity to abundance, from few job opportunities and ways to make a living to economic independence, from religious control to greater possibilities to make one's own choices. Although the contrast between these two worlds had been great before the war, the contrast became even larger for the group who migrated in the first ten years after the war had ended.

Although the material and cultural contrast was great, Jenny and the other newly arrived immigrant women from Agder learned quickly, and it did not take long before they managed the new urban landscape. They walked the streets of Brooklyn in high heels, added more and more English words and expressions to their vocabulary, navigated the city by bus and subway, and entered the shopping malls in downtown Brooklyn, which had once been so unfamiliar. Their arrival in America was the start of a learning process, and new spaces and areas of the metropolis were continuously embodied.

The young women often found their future husbands in America, as had generations of young Agder women before them. Many of them met their husbands in the Norwegian community in Brooklyn, often migrants from the same hometown or another place in Agder. Many of the women who married men from Agder returned to Norway after some years in America. Others married second- or third-generation Norwegians or Americans with other ethnic and national backgrounds. These women rarely returned to Norway.

The women who returned to Agder brought with them new perspectives and knowledge, new clothes and other material culture that differed from what they had back home. Because they had lived in America, they received admiration and respect, and were allowed to oppose some of the norms back home. However, they had to walk a thin line. If they talked too much about life in America, or exaggerated their habits and manners, it would not be seen in the same positive way. Although life in New York gave the young women more freedom and the chance to choose how to live their lives, this was a flexible freedom. Upon their return to Norway, they brought with them parts of their lifestyles, while they left other parts behind in Brooklyn. Nevertheless, having been to America gave the returned migrant women the authority to introduce new perspectives, material culture, and traditions. Their neighbors and friends often excused them for their unconventional behavior because they had been to America. In this manner, the returned migrant women participated in transforming the culture in Agder.

Siv Ringdal *is a cultural historian who has worked on the topic of transatlantic relations between Norway and America for several years. This work has included the curation of exhibitions, the defense of her PhD dissertation in 2016, and the publication of* På høye hæler i Amerika. Unge Agder-kvinner i etterkrigsårenes New York *(On high heels in America: Young Agder women in postwar New York). She is currently a senior curator at the Norwegian Folk Museum in Oslo.*

NOTES

1. This story is referred to in the following two publications: Siv Ringdal, *På høye hæler i Amerika. Unge Agder-kvinner i etterkrigsårenes New York* (Oslo, 2018); *Kroppens transformasjoner blant unge Agder-kvinner i New York, 1945–1965* (Oslo, 2016). I conducted one interview with Jenny in 2010 and followed up with several phone interviews in the time span of 2010–2018.
2. Jenny Solaas changed her surname to Hansen upon marriage.
3. In this article, I define "young women" to be from the age of fifteen to their early twenties. In the Lutheran State Church of Norway, young adults were confirmed the same year they turned fifteen. In the time I am dealing with, confirmation was in many ways synonymous with the entrance to adulthood. I have chosen to focus on this group because I wanted to study these women on their own premises. I wanted to shed light on the young women's motivations for emigrating. Did they have different motivations than men? Although many young, unmarried women migrated to the urban centers of America from the 1880s and forward, there has not been much research on this group. The group is, of course, mentioned in several standard works in the field, for instance in Ingrid Semmingsen's "Veien Mot Vest : [2] : Utvandringen Fra Norge 1865–1915" (Aschehoug, 1950), 498; Odd S. Lovoll's *Det løfterike landet* (Universitetsforlaget, 1997), and in works about Norwegians in different urban centers, such as Odd S. Lovoll's *A Century of Urban Life: The Norwegians in Chicago before 1930* (Northfield, Minn., 1988); and David C. Mauk's *The Colony That Rose from the Sea: The Norwegians in the Red Hook Section of Brooklyn, 1850–1910* (Northfield, Minn., 1991). But there have been few studies that have turned attention on young, female Norwegian immigrants. Some works have partly dealt with this group, such as Janet E. Rasmussen's *New Land New Lives, Scandinavian Immigrants to the Pacific Northwest* (Northfield, Minn., 1993); and Lori Ann Lahlum and Betty Ann Bergland's *Norwegian-American Women: Migration, Communities, and Identities* (St. Paul, Minn., 2011).
4. In 2016 I defended my PhD thesis in cultural history, "Kroppens transformasjoner blant unge Agder-kvinner i New York, 1946–1965," at the University of Oslo (the thesis is in Norwegian but translated to English the title would be "Bodily transformations among young Agder women in New York, 1946–1965). In this PhD thesis I studied a group of young women from the Agder region in Norway who emigrated in the two decades following the Second World War. The main issue was to study how these young women's bodies became a tool they used to negotiate and interpret their transformation from one culture to another. In 2018 I published the book *På høye hæler i Amerika,* which illuminated the same theme, but in which the text was facilitated for a broader audience.
5. In my PhD thesis, twenty-three women were interviewed. In the book, I focused on sixteen women and their stories. The interviews were conducted between 2010 and 2015. Some of the women were interviewed once, others twice. I also followed up with several of the women with questions on the phone. At the time I interviewed them, some of the women had returned to Norway, while others still lived in the United States. Ten of the women I interviewed migrated from 1945–1955, the time span this article deals with. The oldest of the informants was born in 1924, while the youngest was born in 1937.

6. In addition to the qualitative interviews, I also studied a large amount of additional source material from contemporary newspapers, magazines, and moral and beauty books. I also documented photos and material culture.
7. The academic subject of cultural history is relatively new in Norway. The name of the scholarly tradition I am a part of was formerly called ethnology.
8. Bjarne Rogan, "Fra gjenstandsforskning til kulturens materialitet," in *Etnologi og folkloristikk: En fagkritisk biografi om norsk kulturhistorie,* ed. Rogan and Eriksen (Oslo, 2013), 563–65.
9. Bodily and material perspectives have not been the highest priority in Norwegian-American migrant studies and are quite rare. Most of these studies have been related to the study of traditional Norwegian arts and crafts and how they were held alive or gradually abandoned in the new immigrant life. The studies among these that I have found most useful have been the ones about Norwegian-American women, their dress costumes and how they were affected by new life in America, such as Patricia Williams' study from 1993 and Carol Colburn's study from 1994: Patricia J. Williams, "From Folk to Fashion: Norwegian Immigrant Women in the Midwest," in *Dress in American Culture,* ed. Patricia J. Williams, Susan Voso Lab, and Patricia A. Cunningham (Bowling Green, Ohio, 1993); Carol Colburn, "'Well, I Wondered When I Saw You, What All These New Clothes Meant': Interpreting the Dress of Norwegian-American Immigrants," in *Material Culture and People's Art among the Norwegians in America,* ed. Marion John Nelson (Northfield, Minn., 1994). In my study of young women emigrating to urban America in the era of industrialization and consumerism, I have therefore looked to other studies, including studies of other migrant groups. For instance, the works of historian Elizabeth Ewen and historian Barbara A. Schreier, both about young Jewish immigrant women in America, are examples of these works of inspiration: Elizabeth Ewen, *Immigrant Women in the Land of Dollars: Life and Culture on the Lower East Side, 1890–1925* (New York, 1985); Barbara A. Schreier, *Becoming American Women: Clothing and the Jewish Immigrant Experience, 1880–1920* (Chicago, 1995). I have also found inspiration in the works of social historian Joan Jacob Brumberg (1998), cultural historian Kathy Peiss (1998), historian Peter Stearns (1999), media historian Stuart Ewen (1992), and cultural historian Jackson Lears (1994). Several of these scholars deal with immigrants in urban America in different ways, and they have also given me important insight into phenomenon and cultural processes that were central at the time the young Agder women came to New York: Joan Jacobs Brumberg, *The Body Project: An Intimate History of American Girls* (New York, 1998); Kathy Peiss, *Hope in a Jar: The Making of America's Beauty Culture,* 1st ed. (New York: Metropolitan Books, 1998); Peter N. Stearns, *Battleground of Desire: The Struggle for Self-Control in Modern America* (New York, London, 1999); Stuart Ewen and Elizabeth Ewen, *Channels of Desire: Mass Images and the Shaping of American Consciousness* (New York, 1992); T. J. Jackson Lears, *Fables of Abundance: A Cultural History of Advertising in America* (New York, 1994).
10. Paul Basu and Simon Coleman, "Introduction: Migrant Worlds, Material Cultures," *Mobilities* 3 (2008): 328.
11. Setha Low, "Anthropological Theories of Body, Space, and Culture," *Space and Culture* 6:1 (2003): 10.

12. Tine Damsholt, "How Towels Came to Matter: On Discursive-Material Reconfigurings of Gender in Academia," *Kvinder, køn og forskning* 1–2 (2012), 94.
13. Even Lange, *Samling om felles mål: 1935–1970,* ed. Knut Helle et al., vol. 11, Aschehougs Norgeshistorie (Oslo: Aschehoug, 1998), 154–75.
14. This type of migration has been given several names. Migrants temporarily traveling to urban industrial centers from less-developed countries or areas have often been named "labor migrants" or "birds of passage" (Michael J. Piore, *Birds of Passage: Migrant Labour and Industrial Societies* [Cambridge, 1979]). From the Agder area it had been common to cross national and cultural borders to work for a period of time before the local migration to America started. In the seventeenth and eighteenth centuries, before industrialization, several Agder inhabitants migrated to the Netherlands to live and work. The men were most often employed in the maritime sector while the women worked as maids. Several historians and ethnologists have studied this migration, for instance: Sølvi Sogner, *"Og skuta lå i Amsterdam": Et glemt norsk innvandrersamfunn i Amsterdam 1621–1720* (Oslo, 2012); Kariin Sundsback, *Norwegian Women's Migration to Amsterdam and Hoorn, 1600–1750: Life Experiences, Social Mobility and Integration* (Saarbrücken, 2012); Cæcilie Stang, *Arbeidsvandring og utvandring fra kystbygda Feda i Vest-Agder ca. 1750–1950* (Oslo, 1983); Sølvi Sogner, *Ung i Europa* (Oslo, 1994). In the era of migration to the Netherlands, it was also common that migrants returned after some time, with their savings and new knowledge and habits.
15. Before 2020, Agder was divided in two counties, Aust-Agder in the east, and Vest-Agder in west. In this text I will write about Agder as two counties, since this was the situation when the young women left. Traditionally, Agder has referred to both these two counties, but also a historical district in Norway. This district has also been called Sørlandet (south country).
16. "Museumsbulletinen," in *Museumsbulletinen,* ed. Norsk Folkemuseum (Oslo, 2016); Olav Bø, *Setesdal: Folk, kunst og tradisjon* (Oslo, 1980).
17. Johan H. Kloster, "Sjømann-Fisker-Bonde: En Sjøbruksstudie Fra Hidra i Vest-Agder" (Oslo, 1975); *Norsk Sjøfart,* ed. Brit Berggreen et al. (Oslo, 1989).
18. Kåre Rudjord, *Bygdehistorie: Fra formannskapslov til kommunesammenslåing* (Farsund, 1987), 89,155.
19. Rudjord, *Bygdehistorie,* 420–22.
20. Margit Løyland, *Fjordfolk* (Kvinesdal, 1999), 260, 82.
21. "Ekteskap, fødsler og vandringer i Norge 1865–1960," in *Samfunnsøknomiske studier,* ed. Julie Backer (Oslo, 1965).
22. Rudjord, *Bygdehistorie,* 294.
23. Siv Ringdal, *Det amerikanske Lista, Med 110 volt i Huset* (Oslo, 2002).
24. Mauk, *The Colony That Rose from the Sea.*
25. Siv Ringdal, *Lapskaus Boulevard: Et gjensyn med det norske Brooklyn* (Oslo, 2007), 32; Knight Eugene Hoover, *Organizational Networks and Ethnic Persistence: A Case Study of Norwegian-American Ethnicity in the New York Metropolitan Area* (New York, 1983).
26. On 9 April 1940, the German Nazi regime invaded Norway. The country was under German rule for five years, until 8 May 1945. During these years, the inhabitants felt the presence of the German soldiers and the Nazi regime. Kjell-Olav Masdalen, *Agders historie* (Laget,

1991). The occupiers considered the southern coast of Norway to be an area where the Allied forces would likely come to shore in a possible future attack. The Nazi occupiers built up a massive defense system, with bunkers, canons, and forts along the coastal line. During the war, British bomber planes attacked this defense wall on a regular basis. Rudjord, *Bygdehistorie,* 563–87.

27. Masdalen, *Agders historie,* 349–54.
28. For instance, on the peninsula of Lista, where the Germans had established a massive defense system as well as an airport, many had to leave their homes during parts of the war. In some villages and communities, most of the population left and found temporary homes elsewhere, while in other more peaceful areas, the population doubled. In the local primary school on Borhaug at Lista, there were only 5 out of 115 pupils left, and the school had to close. On the other hand, in the small primary school of Eitland, also on Lista, the number of students rose from ten to twenty-one. Rudjord, *Bygdehistorie,* 592.
29. Guri Hjeltnes, "Hverdagsliv under Andre Verdenskrig," https://www.norgeshistorie.no/andre-verdenskrig/hus-og-hjem/1703-hverdagsliv-under-andre-verdenskrig-.html; Masdalen, *Agders historie*, 357–79.
30. Phone interview with Jenny, March 2014.
31. Phone interview with Jenny, March 2014.
32. When I use the term "the church" in the article I refer to the Norwegian Lutheran State Church.
33. Ringdal, *På høye hæler i Amerika,*157.
34. "Amerikanerinnen klær seg ungt," *Alle Kvinners Blad,* 17 November 1945.
35. "Amerikanerinnen klær seg ungt," 17 November 1945.
36. "I Silke Fra Himmelen," *Alle Kvinners Blad,* 17 November 1945.
37. Lange, *Samling om felles mål, 1935–1970* (Oslo, 1998), 159–61.
38. Christine Myrvang, Sissel Myklebust, and Brita Brenna, *Temmet eller uhemmet, Historiske perspektiver på konsum, kultur og dannelse* (Oslo, 2004), 313–14.
39. *Alle Kvinners Blad,* 4 April 1953.
40. Ringdal, *Kroppens transformasjoner blant unge Agder-kvinner i New York,* 145–58.
41. Myrvang, Myklebust, and Brenna, *Temmet eller uhemmet,* 313.
42. Ringdal, *Det amerikanske Lista*; Siv Ringdal and Kjetil Fallan, "110 Volts at Home: The American Lista," *Journal of Design History* 27:1 (2014).
43. Ringdal, *Det amerikanske Lista,* 115–27.
44. Robert E. Park and Herbert A. Miller, *Old World Traits Transplanted* (New York, 1921).
45. Ringdal, *Det amerikanske Lista,* 30.
46. Ringdal, *Det amerikanske Lista,* 46–55.
47. Ringdal, *Det amerikanske Lista*, 228.
48. Phone interview with Jenny, March 2014.
49. Ringdal, *Det amerikanske Lista,* 211–30.
50. Rebecca M. Herzig, *Plucked: A History of Hair Removal* (New York, 2015), 126.
51. In fact, because of their chemical compositions, artificial textiles like nylon will have much brighter colors than if one dyed cotton textiles. Audra J. Wolfe, "Nylon: A Revolution in Textiles," *Chemical Heritage* 26:3 (2008).
52. Ringdal, *På høye hæler i Amerika,* 164.

53. Ringdal, *Det amerikanske Lista,* 187–210.
54. Ringdal, *På høye hæler i Amerika,* 164–66.
55. Phone interview with Jenny, March 2014.
56. Ringdal, *På høye hæler i Amerika,* 152–53.
57. Ringdal, *På høye hæler i Amerika,* 130.
58. Ringdal, *På høye hæler i Amerika,* 63–64.
59. Interview with Jenny, August 2010.
60. Kari Gaupeland changed her surname to Petersen upon marriage.
61. Ringdal, *På høye hæler i Amerika,* 103.
62. Ringdal, *På høye hæler i Amerika,* 105.
63. Ringdal, *På høye hæler i Amerika,* 119.
64. Ringdal, *Lapskaus Boulevard,* 62.
65. Ringdal, *På høye hæler i Amerika,* 176–83.
66. Ringdal, *Kroppens transformasjoner blant unge Agder-kvinner i New York,* 168–69.
67. Pål Repstad and Jan-Olav Henriksen, *Mykere kristendom?: Sørlandsreligion i endring* (Bergen, 2005), 26–28; Bjørg Seland, "Egdene og 'Det ellevte bud,' Kristelig normverk på 18- og 1900-tallet" (Kristiansand, 2008), 85–86; Bjørg Seland and Olaf Aagedal, *Vekkelsesvind: Den norske vekkingskristendomen* (Oslo, 2008), 17–29.
68. Ringdal, *På høye hæler i Amerika,* 324–26.
69. I have been inspired to use the term "choreography" by an article by Charis Cussins. Charis Cussins, "Ontological Choreography: Agency through Objectification in Infertility Clinics," *Sociological Studies of Science* 26:3 (1996), 575. In my PhD thesis I used the term to illuminate how the young women maneuvered between Christian rules and norms and a more secular lifestyle. Ringdal, *Kroppens transformasjoner blant unge Agder-kvinner i New York,* 302–34.
70. Ringdal, *På høye hæler i Amerika,* 339.
71. In the first decade after the Second World War there were about twenty-five Norwegian congregations in the Norwegian community in New York. They represented a broad spectrum of creeds, from the more liberal evangelical Lutheran churches to the more conservative Lutheran free churches, Pentecostals, Methodist churches, and Mission churches. Our Saviors Norwegian Lutheran Church, Norwegian Lutheran Trinity Church, and Zion Norwegian Lutheran Church were popular evangelical Lutheran churches. First Evangelical Free Church (Sixty-Sixth Street Church) and Norwegian Evangelical Lutheran Free Church (Fifty-Ninth Street Church) were popular free churches. Ringdal, *Lapskaus Boulevard,* 84.
72. Ringdal, *På høye hæler i Amerika,* 337–43.
73. Det Norske Folkedanslaget (the Norwegian Folk Dance Group) was originally part of the organization Bondeungdomslaget (BUL), an organization for rural youth that was founded in Brooklyn in 1925. After some years, BULs dance group broke out and established Det Norske Folkedanslaget as an independent dance group. The leader was Åsmund Gøytil, the same man who had established BUL and who had been leading the dance group. In 1948 Det Norske Folkedanslaget had one hundred members. The group performed at the Metropolitan Opera on several occasions, one time with president Roosevelt as part of the audience. Hallvard Bergwitz, "Ein Verdig Ambassadør for Noreg: Leikleidaren Åsmund Gøytil Fekk St. Olavs-Medalja," *Norsk Tidende,* 24 March 1948.

74. Ringdal, *Lapskaus Boulevard,* 146–47.

75. In the postwar era there were two beauty contests held in the Norwegian community in Brooklyn. They were called Miss Norway and Viking Queen. The first precursor of the Viking Queen was crowned in the fall of 1953, while the first Miss Norway was crowned in the fall of 1954. "Festlig, Interessant 'Norway Day' På Women's International Exhibition," *Nordisk Tidende,* 29 October 1953. Ringdal, *Kroppens transformasjoner blant unge Agder-kvinner i New York,* 273–96.

76. In Norway it was common that the salons did both the bride's hair and her makeup on her wedding day.

77. Interview with Jenny, August 2010.

78. Ringdal, *På høye hæler i Amerika,* 342.

A Transatlantic Approach to Teaching and Learning about Norwegian Migration to the United States

Jens Johan Hyvik and Kyle Ward

During the spring semester of 2019 a group of students at Minnesota State University, Mankato (MSU), and the University of South-Eastern Norway (USN)[1] took a course entitled Norwegian Migration to the United States, co-taught by Kyle Ward (MSU) and Jens Johan Hyvik (USN). The course was part of a project funded by Diku (the Norwegian Agency for International Cooperation and Quality Enhancement in Higher Education) under the partnership program for North America. The purpose of this grant was to enable the institutions to offer co-taught courses that students from both universities could enroll in, as well as offer the students a unique educational experience by including Norwegian and American students in the same course. All of this would be done while still allowing students to continue their regular coursework at their home institutions.

In this article, we will discuss the experiences we had creating this course, as well as how the students experienced the course based on their evaluations. In sum: despite needing to overcome several logistical hurdles, the students and professors came away with positive teaching and learning experiences. The hybrid nature of the course, including perhaps most importantly study time in each country, enhanced U.S. and Norwegian students' knowledge of the history of Norwegian migration as well as contributed to their better understanding of Norwegian and American politics and culture more generally.

The Origins of the Course

To begin, it is necessary to discuss the origins of the course and its eventual organization. The first contacts that led to the cooperation between the history departments at MSU and USN were made in 2016 when a delegation from USN (Nils Ivar Agøy, Herleik Baklid, and Jens Johan Hyvik) visited the history faculty at MSU. One of the main reasons the delegation from USN reached out to the faculty at MSU is because these two institutions already had an institutional agreement that allowed for some exchange programs between the two schools. From the start of our meetings in 2016, it seemed like there was a good institutional "match" between MSU and USN, both on an institutional level and an academic level in the respective history departments. MSU and the newly merged USN have approximately the same size student populations and they share a number of similar majors that prepare students for professional jobs. Both MSU and USN's history departments offer history majors, in addition to having a strong focus on teacher education. MSU offers a large social studies education program, as well as a master's program in history, and USN offers a graduate Master of Teacher Education program, or "lektorprogam," in history.

In 2017 the Norwegian Center for Internationalization of Education, SiU (now Diku) published a call for projects under the Partnership Program with North America. Together MSU and USN developed a project we called the Partnership

Program in History. Jens Johan Hyvik was the project manager and coordinator from USN and Kyle Ward served as the coordinator from MSU. The project consisted of two activities: 1. Develop a course about Norwegian emigration to the United States to be co-taught by professors from the two universities and include two study-abroad trips, one to the United States and one to Norway. 2. Run a pilot program where student-teacher candidates from MSU could have a field experience teaching in a Norwegian school and Norwegian students who wanted to go to Minnesota could similarly gain classroom experience. To meet the demands of the teacher exchange, Nøtterøy High School and Mankato West High School were included in the project as Network Partners.

While the focus of this article is the development of the Norwegian Migration to the United States course, it is worth mentioning that the student-teacher exchange has been far more successful than we originally expected. Our hope was to send one student each way, but by the end of the program on March 1, 2020, a total of seven American and four Norwegian students have completed the student-teacher exchange, and the participating schools, the universities, and the cooperating teachers and students have all participated in the program with a lot of enthusiasm.

We received funding from Diku for the project, which resulted in several program-planning meetings held in both the United States and in Norway. In Fall 2018 we welcomed the first group of MSU students who did part of their field teaching experience at Nøtterøy High School. This was followed by two USN students going to Minnesota in 2019 where they primarily worked at Mankato West High School. In the spring term of 2019 we welcomed both MSU and USN students to the Norwegian Migration to the United States course.

The Course: Norwegian Migration to the United States

After much discussion, the decision was made to title the course Norwegian Migration to the United States. Giving the class this specific title helped the professors include both the emigration and immigration aspect of people leaving Norway and settling in the United States. An important part of creating this class was to set up the formal course description, reading list, and curriculum plan for the class. We decided that the course should focus on the period from roughly 1825 to 1925, the first century of Norwegian migration to the United States.

The language of instruction for the course was English, and all the literature for the American students was in English. Odd Lovoll's work *The Promise of America* was the main textbook for the course. We also decided to bring in a fiction book, *Giants in the Earth: A Saga of the Prairie,* by O. E. Rölvaag, which was required reading for all students. The Norwegian students read the same texts in English, in addition to a few texts in Norwegian, most importantly the book *Norsk utvandringshistorie* by Nils Olav Østrem. We choose to include some general readings in American and Norwegian history as well, since we could not expect the students from each country to know much about the history of the other county prior to enrolling in the course.

The students from both universities had the same assignments, which consisted of a midterm written exam and a semester paper, both of which were graded. In the semester paper, the students largely chose their own research topics. In practice this was kind of a compromise, as the American students had fewer graded work requirements than they normally would have had in a course, while the Norwegian students had more work requirements than is often expected in a Norwegian undergraduate-level course in history. However, we found it important that students at both institutions followed more or less the same structure and requirements when possible. In addition to these work requirements, the Norwegian students also had a four-hour written exam at the end of the semester.

The instructional methods for this class were primarily lecture-based and included more or less one lecture a week, all using the online video-conference software OmniJoin. During the lectures, there was time allotted for questions and discussion, but because of the limitations of the video-conference method, lectures by the professors predominated. We had decided that attendance at the lectures was mandatory, to ensure the students would get a chance to get to know one another, and to hear the same lectures for future discussions. The lectures were "live" and were scheduled to start at 8:00 a.m. CST/3:00 p.m. CET to accommodate the time difference between Mankato and Norway.

In addition to attending lectures, students in the course were offered the opportunity to participate in two one-week-long study trips throughout the course of the semester: one to Norway and one to Mankato. When students from both institutions were together during their study exchange trips they engaged in research, participated in discussions, and attended lectures given by faculty at MSU and USN as well as local experts. Ward and Hyvik were involved in all the lectures and classes to provide continuity. While students were required to attend the online lectures, the study exchange trips could not be made mandatory (at least for USN students) in order to comply with Norwegian education law. Norwegian law states that studies at a Norwegian public university should be free from tuition and other costs. It is possible for students to pay for study trips, but the study trips cannot be a requirement of completing the course.

Thanks to the funding from Diku, we were able to sponsor the trips for the students and faculty involved in this class. Along with Diku funding, MSU was also able to offer some funding through grants from the Sons of Norway and the University. While housing, food, and some local transportation costs were covered for all students, they still had to pay for their own plane tickets.

For the Norwegian students, the main destination of the trip to the United States was Mankato, Minnesota. But we also included a full day field trip to Vesterheim, the National Norwegian-American Museum and Heritage Center in Decorah, Iowa, and spent the last day of the trip in Minneapolis-St. Paul visiting the Minnesota Historical Society. We were particularly grateful for the wonderful cooperation with Vesterheim Museum, both for welcoming us to the museum and for giving us a great deal of access to their resources and expertise on this subject. Students in this class were also able to listen to an online lecture given by Vesterheim's curator, Laurann Gilbetson, when she joined the class later to discuss her area of expertise.

The Norwegian students traveled to the United States in March, and were welcomed by an extremely cold Minnesota, where winter still was hanging on. However, the cold weather was soon forgotten as they were greeted by members of the local Sons of Norway lodge in Mankato, who had arranged a welcome dinner (traditional Norwegian-American style) the evening they arrived. The welcome dinner allowed our students the opportunity to discuss the similarities and differences between what Americans and Norwegians view as "traditional" food. Also, Professor Nils Ivar Agøy from USN gave a guest lecture that was well appreciated.

In May the American students traveled to Norway. The main location for the trip was Bø in Telemark and the USN campus there, but the students also spent time in Oslo visiting the Norwegian Museum of Cultural History. While in Telemark the students also went on a one-day field trip to Rjukan and Rauland. Rjukan is known in Norwegian emigration history for its early and substantial emigration. Then, at the USN campus in Rauland, the students were introduced to Norwegian folk culture and music, as well as traditional food. We discovered that having the students from both countries share in these field trips and cultural opportunities allowed for the class to have some great discussions regarding immigration and transference of cultural, social, political, and religious aspects from one country to another.

Figure 1. American and Norwegian students at University of South-Eastern Norway–Campus Bø in May 2019. Photograph by author Kyle Ward.

Logistical Challenges

On the way to actually getting the course up and running we had to deal with several challenges. Some of them we had dealt with already in the project application to Diku, others we had to deal with later on. The first challenge was how to organize the formalities of the course. Which institution should offer the course (and grant the credits to the students)? In the project proposal, we had already decided that each institution would establish a course at their home institution and award the credits for their own students. The main reason for this was due to the different grading systems.

Second, how many students should participate in the course? In the project proposal, we set the limit at ten students from each institution. This had a lot to do with practicalities. We wanted a group that was not too big since this was the first time the course was being offered, and there were practical limitations when it came to arranging the study-abroad trips. In the end, we ended up with eleven American and seven Norwegian students enrolled in the course.

Third, we realized in the planning process that we could not award the same amount of credits to the two student groups because of the way the programs at their home institutions are set up. Therefore, the MSU course became a 4-credit course (7.5 ECTS credits), while the USN course was 15 Norwegian and ECTS credits. Accordingly, the Norwegian students were expected to read more literature, and they had to have a four-hour written exam at the end of the semester.

Fourth, the aim of the course was to have lectures by faculty from both USN and MSU available online. Just to get the technicalities to work properly proved quite difficult, and we used several meetings involving technical support staff from both institutions to decide on a video-conference program that worked well. After agreeing to the best video-conferencing system (OmniJoin), we still had to deal with the logistical challenges of running the actual classes. While the American students, to a large extent, met in a classroom at MSU, and watched the lectures together, the Norwegian students followed the lectures from their personal computers. This was because the Norwegian students belonged both to campus Bø and Vestfold at USN, as well as students enrolled in online study programs. However, after we decided on the video-conference program and started up the lectures, the technicalities worked out well. That is not to say there were not any problems, but all in all it worked, and there were not many complaints from either the students or teachers.

An additional issue that came up during course development was related to scheduling. While the syllabi for both the USN and MSU classes were almost identical, there was one issue that was initially overlooked, and that was that the public (and academic) calendars in Norway and the United States are quite different from one another. In Norway, there are some days off, most of them because of religious holidays, while in the United States there are fewer religious-based holidays, but other secular ones, like spring break and Martin Luther King Day. Another scheduling issue that we did not think about while planning the course was related to the fact that in Norway students typically have a much longer final exam period. The study trip for the American students to Norway was arranged in the middle of the exam period for the Norwegian students in May. In the end, everyone attended the exams they had to attend, but it created certain challenges for those Norwegian students having exams in other classes.

The Student Experience

By the end of the study trip in Norway, we challenged the students to write down the three main things they learned, or would remember in the future, from taking this course. We also had a classroom session where we discussed and evaluated the course. The reactions from these students was overwhelmingly positive, and some main themes occurred:

1. Students believed they had learned a lot about the reasons Norwegians emigrated as well as how they created new communities in the United States. Several mentioned in particular that they felt the work with the semester paper had been very valuable.
2. Students were particularly happy with reading *Giants in the Earth* and felt the novel had contributed positively to their experience. They believed that the novel gave them another kind of perspective on the topic than what they got from the

other literature. The immigrant's life and experiences seemed to be made more real for them.

3. Students felt they learned a great deal about each other's country and felt they had a better cultural and political understanding of the United States and Norway.
4. Students believed that actually visiting the other country, meeting with experts, and visiting museums/historic sites had a great impact on their understanding of the course content.
5. Students were able to compare historic Norwegian immigration to what is happening today in terms of immigration around the world. Comments were made about the impact that societal forces have on why people emigrate and how strong the Norwegian identity still is in parts of the United States to this day.

Figure 2. American and Norwegian students visit the medieval church in Bø in May 2019. Dr. Herleik Baklid (USN) informs the students about the church and its history. Photograph by author Kyle Ward.

Teacher Experiences

From a teacher standpoint, our experience was that the students who decided to take the course were generally committed, completed their readings, and actively participated. The starting point for the students in this regard was probably different for the two groups, as American students in general are expected to participate in their classes in a more active way than Norwegians. However, it turned out that we did not experience a big difference with the students in this regard, either in the online lectures or on the study trips. The student groups easily mingled with one another on the study trips and got to know each other quite well.

One area where things did not work as well as we wanted, was in having the students do academic work together. Initially we planned to put the students in groups based on the topics of their semester papers. We made an effort to make this work, but since the papers had to be written individually, and the students chose to write about many different topics, it proved difficult for this to work well. From the feedback we got from the students, they still were very happy about writing semester papers and learned a lot from it. However, several suggested we could have initiated a mandatory but ungraded group project, which would have mixed Americans and Norwegians together early on in the semester. Students expressed an interest in working together early on so that they could get to know each other better before the study-abroad trips. This is an idea we would like to develop further if we teach the course again.

Because of airplane departure and arrival times and prices as well as other circumstances, we also had to limit the number of days spent in both the United States and Norway. A few more days at the MSU and USN campuses would have been nice. These extra days would have allowed students to engage in more group work as well as give them more time to work individually on their semester papers. This additional time spent on their individual research would have given students the chance to get to know the resources found on each campus better, especially in terms of using the libraries. These extra days also would have allowed the students more time to socialize and get to know each other.

During the course, we brought in several faculty members from both USN and MSU to give guest lectures. In many ways, this was very successful, as the students met with experts in the field. It is hard to mention only a few, as so many participated in such a generous way and had wonderful lectures, but the lectures on immigrant women by Dr. Lori Lahlum during the study trip to Mankato, Dr. Melissa Gjellstad (University of North Dakota), who joined the class online, and professor Øyvind Gulliksen's lecture about Rölvaag's *Giants in the Earth* and immigrant letters during the study trip to Norway deserve to be mentioned.

We hope to be able to offer the course again in the future and are considering different ways to make this possible. We would ideally offer it every third year, as the course requires extra planning and special arrangements. A challenge however is the funding, as we probably need external funding to make the study trips economically feasible for the students. Another possibility we are considering is to run the course without the study trips, as a transatlantic online course. This option is less appealing as it would not offer students the same unique experience. The study trips, and the direct contact they make possible between students both in and outside the classroom, are of great value. We are also considering ways to use the online-based model we developed for this course to offer more joint courses between USN and MSU.

Jens Johan Hyvik *is Professor of Modern History at University of South-Eastern Norway, Department of Business, History and Social Sciences, School of Business. He has published several books and articles about Norwegian nationalism in the long nineteenth century.*

Kyle Ward *is the Director of Social Studies Education at Minnesota State University, Mankato, where he also teaches history courses. He is the author of five books on history and historiography and a workbook series, which focuses on historical thinking skills for students.*

NOTES

1. In 2016 Telemark University College and Vestfold and Buskerud University College merged. In 2018, the merged institution was granted status as a University.

REVIEWS

David M. Krueger, *Myths of the Rune Stone: Viking Martyrs and the Birthplace of America* (Minneapolis: University of Minnesota Press, 2015). 232 pages.

Dag Blanck

In the late summer of 1898 the Swedish-born farmer Olof Öhman discovered a slab of stone while pulling tree stumps on his farm in Douglas County in central Minnesota, not far from the town of Kensington. The strange markings found on the stone's surface attracted immediate attention. They were interpreted as Nordic runes conveying the message that in 1362, thirty Swedes and Norwegians had traveled west from the Vinland settlement on the North American east coast to present-day Minnesota, where they had made camp and engaged in struggles with the Native population.

Ever since its discovery, the Kensington Rune Stone, as it has become known, has been a source of great attention. In fact, Henrik Williams, a leading runologist at Uppsala University, has called it "the most famous of all [runestones]"[1] It has been the subject of a century-long controversy over whether the stone dates from 1362. If true, this would mean that the history of European-American relations must be rewritten and the first European settlements in the present-day United States be placed in Minnesota in the 1360s instead of in Virginia and Massachusetts in the decades after 1608. The stone has been examined by a number of scholars from both sides of the Atlantic since 1899. From the very beginning the overwhelming scholarly consensus has been that it is not a medieval inscription, but that it dates from the late 1890s, which means that it does not prove that Scandinavians reached Minnesota in 1362. Still, and in the face of overwhelming evidence, the question has never faded and arguments keep being made for the stone's "authenticity."

There is an extensive literature about the Kensington stone, focusing on the question of authenticity (is it a medieval inscription?) and on the history of the stone in general (its discovery and who made the inscription). Too little systematic attention has been paid to the question of why the inscription was made and to the ideological and symbolic role it has played. *Myths of the Rune Stone* seeks to remedy that situation.

In the book's six chapters, Kruger proposes different ways of understanding why the stone was made and why beliefs in its message have endured to the present day. One important theme is how the stone made it possible to argue for an early Swedish and/or Scandinavian presence in the United States. During the latter half of the nineteenth century several Scandinavian-American intellectuals began arguing that the Vikings had been the first Europeans to reach North America and what is today the United States. Krueger points to Rasmus B. Anderson, professor of Scandinavian languages at the University of Wisconsin, as "the first widely known writer to promote the myth of Viking discovery" (18). In Anderson's *America Not Discovered by Columbus* (1874) he challenged the predominant Anglo-Saxon historiography, instead placing Norwegians and Scandinavians center stage as the first Europeans in North America. The wish to establish an early presence by using history to legitimize the contemporary immigrant group's status in the United States can be found among most European immigrants in the late nineteenth century. The Vikings were frequently invoked by Scandinavian Americans, and Kreuger places the Kensington stone in a larger discussion of other examples of purported remnants of a Viking past in the United States, such as the tower in Newport, Rhode Island, the Dighton Rock inscription near Fall River, Massachusetts, or the sailing of a replica of a Norwegian Viking ship to the Columbian Exposition in Chicago in the summer of 1893. It should be noted that similar claims to the Vikings were made by Swedish Americans at the same time, most notably by Johan Enander, and that Scandinavian Americans thus engaged in what historian Jean M. O'Brien has called "firsting."[2] Krueger is also wise in placing the runestone and Scandinavian immigrants in the ethno-racial hierarchies of late nineteenth century America.

A second theme concerns religion. Krueger notes that the narrative surrounding the runestone not only concerned an early presence but also, and increasingly, came to include a religious element. If Scandinavian Vikings had reached Minnesota in 1362 they would have been pre-Reformation travelers and thus Catholics. This created a tension for the overwhelmingly Lutheran Scandinavian immigrants in the late nineteenth century, many of whom had embraced the American anti-Catholicism of the mid-nineteenth century. Krueger notes how both Rasmus Anderson and Johan Enander carefully omit the specific denominational nature of the alleged Norse presence in the United States and instead refer to them as generically "Christian" (94).

The Catholicism of the Vikings was, however, not lost on the Minnesota Catholic community in the late nineteenth century. In an elegant and carefully argued discussion, Krueger shows how Bishop John Ireland of Minnesota's growing Catholic community was able to claim the runestone as a "Catholic American artifact" (96) and use it as a part of missionary activities among Scandinavian Americans in Minnesota. Furthermore, Krueger shows how the memory of the Catholic Vikings was used in the dedication of a Catholic elementary school in Alexandria, Minnesota, in 1957 and how they became a part of the ideological Cold War between the United States and the Soviet Union.

A third factor for understanding the durability of the myths of the runestone is its role as a civic artifact. The runestone and the Runestone Museum, established in 1958, have served to create a regional and civic identity that transcends the ethnic and religious elements. Krueger uses Odd Lovoll's term "chamber of commerce ethnicity" as a way of describing the combination of business and tourism interests that have also shaped the understanding of the Kensington stone (chapter 1, note 90). The runestone's display in the Minnesota Pavilion during the New York World's Fair in 1965, replete with a visit by Vice President Humphrey, an interview with Alexandria Mayor Marvin Hansen on the NBC *Today Show,* and the twenty-eight foot statute of a Viking outside the pavilion carrying a shield with the inscription "Minnesota: Birthplace of America?" further solidified the runestone's position as a both a Minnesotan and an American artifact.

David Kruger has written an important book about the Kensington runestone and about how history is used and abused. Its strength lies in going beyond the "authenticity" controversy and discussing the runestone's symbolic and ideological roles and the reasons why the persistent belief in the runestone as a medieval artifact has endured. It opens the way for more work, especially on the ways in which Scandinavian Americans became a part of the ethnic and racial hierarchies in late nineteenth- and early twentieth-century America. It also shows how powerful ethnic myths are and how hard it can be to communicate scholarly results that undermine them.

Dag Blanck *is Professor of North American Studies at Uppsala University and director of the Swenson Swedish Immigration Research Center at Augustana College in Rock Island, Illinois. His work is in American immigration history and transnational relations between Sweden and the United States.*

NOTES

1. Henrik Williams, "The Kensington Rune Stone: Fact and Fiction," *Swedish-American Historical Quarterly* 63 (January 2012): 7.
2. Jean M. O'Brien, *Firsting and Lasting: Writing Indians out of Existence in New England* (Minneapolis: University of Minnesota Press, 2010).

Ane-Charlotte Five Aarset, *They Sang for Norway: Olaf Oleson's Immigrant Choir* (St. Paul: Minnesota Historical Society Press, 2017). Pages ix & 266.

James P. Leary

In 1938 Theodore Blegen and Knut Gjerset, distinguished members of the Norwegian-American Historical Association (NAHA) editorial board, urged Olaf Oleson to pen his memoirs. He replied that an already produced half-page summary should suffice. Ane-Charlotte Five Aarset's fine book firmly establishes both the bygone NAHA editors' motives and Oleson's modesty.

Yet some readers may find this book's English-language title misleading. Published as *Utvandreren* (The emigrant) in Norwegian in 2012—perhaps deemed too closely resembling *Utvandrarna* (The Emigrants), the first of Vilhelm Moberg's Swedish-American trilogy—*They Sang for Norway* neither offers a fully realized history of an immigrant choir within the context of Norwegian-American singing societies, nor even mentions such major figures as the composer F. Melius Christiansen, who established the internationally renowned St. Olaf Choir, or Carsten Woll, the most prolific Norwegian-American recording artist and editor of *Sangbog for Sønner af Norge* (Sons of Norway songbook; Minneapolis 1926). Nor do the many songs mentioned throughout the book figure in an otherwise excellent index.

Caveats aside, *They Sang for Norway* succeeds as the long overdue biography of a remarkable emigrant entrepreneur, philanthropist, choral singer and composer, civic-minded American, and tireless advocate for Norwegians in the Old and New Worlds.

Born in Nord-Trøndelag, Olaf Martin Olsen Five (1849–1944) followed his older brother's lead in 1870 by settling in Fort Dodge, Iowa, and swapping the "Five" farm name for the patronymic surname Oleson. Already an accomplished gardener, brilliant and industrious, Oleson acquired pharmacy training, established a business, made savvy investments, and incrementally amassed a considerable fortune, significant parts of which financed his lifelong commitment to Norwegian language and culture. Notably Oleson founded a Norwegian singing group in Fort Dodge in 1872; provided organizational and financial support for the fledgling Norwegian Singers' Association of America in 1892; established an annual prize in literature through *Det Norske Selskab i Amerika* (the Norwegian Society in America) in 1903; used his connections to arrange the first White House concert by visiting Norwegian singers in June 1905 to urge American recognition of Norwegian independence; provided substantial funds to create the Norwegian Singers' Association of America's periodical *Sanger-Hilsen* in 1910; launched a Norwegian-American composer's competition in 1920; helped found the Norwegian-American Historical Association as the first contributor and treasurer in 1925; and was appointed to the Royal Norwegian Order of St. Olaf in 1929 in recognition of "his work for the preservation of Norwegianness in the USA" (194).

Oleson's full life emerges chronologically through fifty-two short chapters, roughly half of which focus on or include music and songs. A lucid writer and able researcher, Aarset draws masterfully upon primary sources (public records, singing society publications, newspaper accounts, letters, memoirs), most of them in Norwegian, as well as a wealth of rare and vivid illustrations from archives on both sides of the Atlantic. Her family connection and Norwegian perspective provide significant dimensions throughout.

As Oleson's great-grandniece, Aarset grew up hearing stories about the uncle who made a fortune in America. She likewise wrote an award-winning biography of her great-grandfather who stayed at home in Nord-Trøndelag: Oleson's brother, Ola Five, the "Marksman General" whose militias aided Norway's independence from Sweden in 1905. Although separated by the north Atlantic and half a continent, the brothers' lives intertwined through correspondence, visits from mutual acquaintances, and steadfast commitments to Norway.

Skillfully telling both sides of an undiminished transatlantic story, Aarset demonstrates how the free exchange of peoples and ideas across borders enriched both nations—especially through Oleson's encounters with such Norwegian artists and intellectuals as Bjørnsterne Bjørnson, Ole Bull, and Edvard Grieg. Aarset likewise illuminates important issues, debates, and paradoxes regarding cultural and linguistic pluralism that emerge, then and now, from the experiences and actions of immigrants.

In part exemplifying a deracinated expatriate embracing a new identity, Olaf Oleson became fluent in English, married across ethnic lines, was active in Democratic Party politics despite Norwegian Americans' overwhelming Republican preference, helped fund a Catholic hospital, and had a Congregationalist rather than Lutheran funeral. Nonetheless, like Irish America's Fenians, Oleson and members of midwestern Norwegian singing societies raised funds and bought weapons to help free their homeland. And Oleson continued to speak, write, sing, and compose songs in Norwegian, espousing the anti-assimilationist sentiment of his friend and Norwegian-language advocate, the novelist and journalist Waldemar Ager: "The prevailing 'melting pot' idea will only result in banality" (180).

James P. Leary *is Emeritus Professor of Folklore and Scandinavian Studies and cofounder of the Center for the Study of Upper Midwestern Cultures at the University of Wisconsin–Madison. His many publications include* So Ole Says to Lena: Folk Humor of the Upper Midwest *(2001), and* Folksongs of Another America *(2015).*

Ola Larsmo, *Swede Hollow* (Minneapolis: University of Minnesota Press, 2019). 310 pages.

Ingeborg Kongslien

This powerful narrative depicts an important part of Swedish-American history through the story of the Klar family and a handful of other individuals who left Sweden just before the turn of the twentieth century to find a new and better life in America. *Swede Hollow* is a novel in that its characters and events are fictional, but the descriptions of the characters' lives and circumstances are based on solid historical research and knowledge. It is thus a historical-documentary novel that contributes new knowledge and insight into Swedish America, in particular about a period and a place that has not been that much featured, either in research or in writing.

Time and place are important structural elements of the novel. The time at the turn of the century constitutes the main part of the book, with short tales from subsequent decades to round off individual life stories. The place is Swede Hollow, the poor ghetto or slum in a ravine on the outskirts of St. Paul, Minnesota, named after the Swedish immigrants who lived in its shacks and polluted environments. They were mainly from working-class backgrounds and in their new lives most had access only to unsteady day labor jobs, often hard and dangerous ones like on the railroad. These circumstances led them to take part in union work and strikes. The perspective offered is consistently from below, from the bottom of society.

The group of characters, with the Klar family of five in the center, have their individual stories presented from their arrival in 1897 and some years on, while scenes from around 1920, the late 1920s, and mid-1930s round off the individual destinies. Two epilogues dated 1956 and 2007 point to the future. The parents toil as well as they can, Gustaf in uncertain and precarious jobs, and Anna holding a home together in their shanty house, but they can never get much beyond a day-to-day subsistence. The young son Carl is weak and gets sick from the unhealthy environment and dies, the oldest sister works hard, climbs socially and economically, and moves away, and the younger sister who is more open to life is left alone with a newborn child to raise, a new Carl. His fate is as bleak and heart-wrenching as can be when he is wrongly accused of having taken part in a lynching, and when finally released from jail, he tries to move ahead but dies in an accident on a freight train. His story is one of the few first-person narratives in the novel, and it ends: "I never held the rope. I never met my father" (269). Tragedy and unfairness are abundant, but the young woman Inga, both a caretaker of people around her and a live wire who even manages to buy her own house, brings in some light.

Larsmo does not evade describing the toils and grimness of these people's lives, but also shows their dignity and compassion as well as their strength and resilience. As a "group novel" with several characters, it adds to representation, and quotations from newspapers of the time add to authenticity and an outside perspective on the Swedish community. A strong narrative voice holds together the many characters and time periods in this book where the main character is actually Swede Hollow itself. The presence of unfairness and a clear class perspective runs throughout the narrative as a whole as well as in the individual tales. My main objection is that there is possibly one tale too many. The crime story of the unhappy couple and the horrible husband, with murder and prison to follow, takes up a disproportionate space, and although it fits in thematically, it is so intense that it possibly leads to overstating the grimness in the novel as a whole.

Swede Hollow combines great knowledge of history with fascinating character descriptions and enthralling life stories in a rich literary language. It echoes Vilhelm Moberg's iconic emigrant epic, but with half a century time difference and an urban versus a rural context. Anyone interested in Scandinavian-American history and culture would greatly appreciate this book and be enriched in knowledge and insight. It adds an important chapter to this history, a part that has not been much in focus earlier. Moreover, with migration and people living at borders being such prevalent features of today, this book will have a wider appeal and relevance. The novel was originally published in Swedish in 2016. The English translation is by Tiina Nunnally, and the quality of the translation equals that of the original.

Ingeborg Kongslien*, Professor Emeritus at the University of Oslo in Scandinavian Studies, specializes in multicultural literature. She has also taught at the University of Chicago, the University of Wisconsin, and Stockholm University.*

Anita Olson Gustafson, *Swedish Chicago: The Shaping of an Immigrant Community, 1880–1920* (Dekalb: Northern Illinois University Press, 2018). 212 pages.

Erika K. Jackson

Ulf Beijbom's *Swedes in Chicago* (1971) is the common starting point for scholars researching the history of Scandinavian Americans in Chicago. His classic work depicts the city's early squatter settlements as disjointed and eventually disintegrating as Swedes moved to suburban regions. Anita Olson Gustafson, a professor of history at Mercer University, begins her study where Beijbom's concludes, arguing that Swedish ethnicity remained strong in the years following 1880 maintained by church and club membership, social affiliations, and other community-building projects. Gustafson's book is the culmination of two decades' worth of important contributions to the historiography of Swedish immigrants and education, community, and ethnic traditions, and influenced by the mentorship of the late H. Arnold Barton.

Swedish Chicago follows a thematic organization, beginning with an examination of immigration patterns in the late nineteenth century, followed by context on the establishment of Swedish-American enclaves. Gustafson acknowledges the distance between the three separate settlements—the farthest separated by twenty-six miles—but reassures her readers that space did not distract from a "complex Swedish-American identity" that combined heritage with "new urban realities" (1). The book's five chapters provide invaluable translations of Swedish-language documents from the Swedish Emigrant Institute in Växjö, Sweden; quantitative data on demographics vital to understanding ethnic composition; and maps and photographs. Chapter 1 contends that Swedish ethnic representation thrived between 1880 and 1920 as evidenced by the establishment of churches and secular clubs. Such institutions offered an expression of a unique Nordic identity that led to the creation of community institutions marked by diverse ideologies. Swedes created a "middle ground" in which moderate assimilation to American customs balanced with ties to home in an effort to adapt to their new urban surroundings (33). Swedes wrote to family and friends about the importance of a strong work ethic, concerns about city dangers and economics, and discussed strategies for adjustment. The book's strongest chapter, "Church Growth in Swedish Chicago," provides quantitative documentation of the origins of Swedish Chicago's church membership. Between 1880 and 1920, church membership grew by nearly 10 percent as Swedes remained committed to the church and involved their children out of a desire to maintain ethnic ties. Immanuel Lutheran instituted Sunday school (an American concept) to educate Swedish-American children in religious traditions, however, there was a growing resistance among youth in adopting their parents' Swedish customs.

Chapter 4 addresses the role of nonsecular and secular clubs in maintaining Swedishness and providing fraternal community. Chicago's Svithiod, Viking Orders, and Swedish sport clubs renewed cultural traditions of singing, athleticism, and theatrical performance in America. Temperance organizations projected a positive image of Swedish workers to Americans who worried about immigrant "fitness" for society. Such groups fostered the growth of Swedish nationalism in Chicago—self-promotion and the belief in cultural exceptionalism—as did the church, the ethnic press, and Swedish-American colleges. Gustafson concludes that nationalism was strong in Sweden, but not as strong as that of self-conscious Chicago Swedes looking to distinguish themselves from other immigrant groups. The epilogue notes that by the 1920s, Swedish Americans living in Chicago, particularly members of Swedish churches, felt the pressures to conform to American customs. Yet today, neighborhoods like Andersonville contain reminders of the old ethnic traditions, even if its businesses are no longer Swedish-owned but rather inspired by Swedish culture.

Gustafson's book provides a useful update to Beijbom's work, though she employs an approach more commonly situated in the historiography of the 1980s and 1990s. Her narrative mentions whiteness in passing, briefly citing Jørn Brøndal's and Dag Blanck's 2014 contributions to the *Journal of American Ethnic History*,[1] but the topic of Nordic whiteness is altogether lacking from discussions of the Swedish ethnic experience in Chicago. Equally absent is critical analysis of race more generally, and gender more specifically. Gustafson retells the rich and compelling stories of her historical actors, though misses opportunities to provide analysis of gender difference or racial conflict between neighbors. This omission is disappointing when considering early battles between Swedes, the Irish, and Italians in Swede Town over religion and social positioning in American society. Further rhetorical analysis into the term "community" would help the reader to better comprehend how an ethnic group spread across a physical urban expanse constituted a cohesive, interconnected group of individuals also divided by religious denomination, class, and generation. These points of critique, however, are small when compared to the readability of *Swedish Chicago*'s narrative. The book offers a clear presentation of the topic and introduces Swedish-American urban history to a wide readership.

Erika K. Jackson *is Associate Professor of History at Colorado Mesa University and author of* Scandinavians in Chicago: The Origins of White Privilege in Modern America *(University of Illinois Press, 2019) and coeditor of* Nordic Whiteness and Migration to the USA: A Historical Exploration of Identity *(Routledge, 2020) with Jana Sverdljuk, Terje Mikael Hasle Joranger, and Peter Kivisto.*

NOTES

1. Jørn Brøndal, "The Fairest among the So-Called White Races: Portrayals of Scandinavian Americans in the Filiopietistic and Nativist Literature of the Late Nineteenth and Early Twentieth Centuries." *Journal of American Ethnic History* 33, no. 3 (Spring 2014): 5–36; Dag Blanck, "A Mixture of People with Different Roots: Swedish Immigrants in the American Ethno-Racial Hierarchies." *Journal of American Ethnic History* 33, no. 3 (Spring 2014): 37–54.

Erika Jackson, *Scandinavians in Chicago: The Origins of White Privilege in America* (Urbana: University of Illinois Press, 2019). Pages xi & 229.

Odd S. Lovoll

The foundation for whiteness studies was laid in 1991 by David Roediger in his book *The Wages of Whiteness* and expanded on later in his study *Working Toward Whiteness*. In the first work he explores the role of racism in the development of the white working class in the nineteenth century; in the second he looks at the situation in the twentieth century and shows how American ethnic groups whose whiteness earlier had been in question gradually gained the status of "white" Americans.[1] According to Peter Kolchin, whiteness studies became a burgeoning field with a wide variety of approaches; he sees the significance of these studies as a new way to show the absurdity of race and racial hierarchy as a system of categorizing humans.[2]

In her well researched and convincingly argued study, Erika K. Jackson places the Scandinavian-American experience within the context of historical whiteness. In a concluding summary, she reiterates the study's major intents, including the socially constructed hierarchy of race and the selection of Chicago, which became an essential backdrop "in illustrating the process by which people of Scandinavian descent became the embodiment of whiteness in the United States between the late nineteenth and early twentieth centuries" (189).

Scandinavians were, however, not initially viewed as approaching the racial status of Americans of Anglo-Saxon heritage. Indeed, from the founding of Chicago in 1837 and to the aftermath of the Chicago fire (1871) they were not seen as a part of a preferred race of people. In the first chapter, Jackson delineates the process in detail of how Scandinavians by the 1880s, preceding popular racial classifications, were moving closer to being considered "old stock" like Americans. In a brief review, it is impossible to consider adequately the varied analytical components of the narrative, such as the natural selection ideology of social Darwinism and its role in racism, the growth of race "science," the role of the World's Columbian Exposition of 1893, and the positive portrayal of

Scandinavians by early historians. What stands out as a major factor is upward social mobility and the resulting prosperity, especially in the construction industry following the Great Fire.

Nordic whiteness, a racial construct, was on full display at the 1893 exposition; the concept thereafter took on importance within the discourse on race. The ethnographic exhibits by the three Scandinavian countries, and the arrival of a replica of a Viking ship, furthered the narrative of white privilege on behalf of Scandinavian Americans and Scandinavians. The Viking ship's sailing symbolized the Vikings' discovery of America and can certainly be regarded as a challenge to the exposition's distinct Columbian commemoration.

The book also delves into pageants that established positive stereotypical opinions of the beauty of Scandinavian women. White privilege extended into the workplace as well, perhaps symbolized by, to cite a chapter title, "The 'Swedish Maid,' [and] 'Strong' Nordic Workers in an Elite American World" (79). Scandinavians were also guilty of vice and criminal activity, but as the Norwegian and Swedish newspapers maintained, to a much lower degree than other immigrant nationalities; by 1900 Chicago was considered one of the most lawless cities in the United States. Anarchy was countered by reform movements. Jackson provides a most enlightening discussion of the Scandinavian-American settlement movement and its extensive progressive social role.

The issue of loyalty and the nativist rhetoric during World War I escalated into mass hysteria after the United States declared war on Germany. Scandinavian Americans in Chicago identified themselves as "Nordic," a term that came into vogue in the 1920s when, according to the book's narrative, "Nordic" became almost interchangeable with "Aryan" (138). In his 1916 work of scientific racism, *The Passing of the Great Race,* eugenicist Madison Grant decreed the Nordic race "the white race par excellence" (136). The Scandinavian-language press, even if not reading Grant's study, used racial discourse that positioned Scandinavians away from the German enemy.

Scandinavians in Chicago witnessed a cultural revival in the 1920s, but one that honored their cultural preference within American society and a dualistic sense of citizenship. The Norwegian community used the 1925 centennial to reflect on its hyphenated American identity. In assessing the contemporary importance of Nordic whiteness, Jackson concludes, to quote: "Today, Nordic whiteness remains as the ultimate position of racial hegemony and privilege" (180), even though, as she explains, Scandinavian ethnicity has become the more politically correct identity by which Americans signify their white privilege.

Scandinavians in Chicago is clearly a major scholarly work within whiteness studies and the topic of white privilege. The undersigned relates well to the author's desire for self-identity as a motivation for writing the book. As a Norwegian immigrant, my own motivation in my research and writing has been an enduring scholarly pursuit to comprehend and explain the immigrant experience. How does moving from a familiar social setting to a foreign one shape the acceptance of a new identity and different cultural and social values? Few challenges are more demanding. It is in this regard I have some concerns about whiteness studies in general. Ronald Bayor, cited also by Jackson, president of the Immigration and Ethnic History Society, in 2009 claimed that a nationality-based ethnic identity is one among other identities and values and that whiteness does not account for the apparent persistence of some ethnic cultural-behavioral patterns. He states, "The conclusion is that a white racial identity has been overstated but does exist, and ethnicity in the form of cultural patterns, values, and behaviors can still be relevant over generations."[3] The final observation is worth keeping in mind.

***Odd S. Lovoll**, the third NAHA editor and first occupant of the King Olav V Chair in Scandinavian-American Studies at St. Olaf College, holds a PhD in United States History with specialization in immigration. He is the author of a number of books and articles, including* A Century of Urban Life: The Norwegians in Chicago before 1930 *(Northfield, Minn.: NAHA, 1988).*

NOTES

1. David R. Roediger, *The Wages of Whiteness,* rev.ed. (New York: Verso, 1999); David R. Roediger, *Working Toward Whiteness* (New York, 2005).
2. Peter Kolchin, "Whiteness Studies: The New History of Race," in the *Journal of American History* (June 2002), 154–73.
3. Ronald R. Bayor, "Another Look at 'Whiteness': The Persistence of Ethnicity in American Life," in *Journal of American Ethnic History* (Fall 2009): 13–30, quote 25.

Kate Allen and John E. Ingulsrud, *The Norwegian-American Lutheran Experience in 1950s Japan: Stepping Up to the Cold War Challenge* (New York: Lexington Books, 2016). Pages. xvii & 313.

Kari G. Hempel

The Norwegian-American Lutheran Experience in 1950s Japan: Stepping Up to the Cold War Challenge by Kate Allen and John E. Ingulsrud briefly introduces Norwegian-American mission work in Japan during the early Cold War years, 1950–1956. The main content deals with Christian missionary activity in Japan during the several hundred years prior, Norwegian Lutheran history in the United States, and the ELC (Evangelical Lutheran Church) as a mission organization, as well as a description of difficult encounters with Japanese culture. The theory used is related to language learning (Japanese) and to cross-cultural exchange.

The empirical material consists of congregational and historical documents. More importantly, it consists of interviews with full-time missionaries and their wives and single missionaries, collected and processed by the authors and previous researchers over fifteen years. The interviews offer personal testimony of encounters with Japanese people and culture. The material shows, not surprisingly, that the encounters differ according to one's position and tasks. Almost every missionary in Japan during the period had experience from the China mission field, before China prohibited Christian missionary activity there. However, this background did not prove to be an advantage. The cultural differences between the Asian nations were too great to benefit from the experience.

Norwegian missionaries often portray Japan as a difficult field, with few conversions compared to the resources used. This book points to the same facts, but regards them differently by emphasizing the qualitative aspects of the mission assignment rather than the quantitative. The different positions formulated through the word pair *Missio Dei* or *Missio Ecclesiae* represent opposite views on mission strategy. *Missio Ecclesiae,* church planting, worked with a goal of making the indigenous churches independent. The working method was a three "self" formula: self-supporting, self-propagating, and self-governing. With a self-supporting indigenous church, the link with the mission organizations became weak, resulting in declining mission interest. The authors seem to recommend future mission strategy in line with the *Missio Dei* thinking, being more ecumenical and less denomination-related, more quality than quantity orientated than is common in Protestant thinking, and more concerned about the culture in the recipient country than previous strategies. I see this as the main argument, despite the fact that the authors are linguists and a significant part of the book is devoted to discussions of language learning and preparation for meeting a new culture.

The discussion is based on a thorough introduction to mission history in Japan, from the Catholic mission of the sixteenth century to Protestant mission history from the 1950s, when the country was opened after 250 years of isolation. As far as the Norwegian-American background is concerned, the description is updated and elaborated. Norwegian Americans established exclusive ethnic churches. Within the integration process, however, they became more inclusive and ecumenical. Perhaps a transnational perspective of Norwegian-American culture could have been highlighted. The gap between a Norwegian and a Norwegian-American culture, albeit both Lutheran, is large.

Recent research on causes of emigration from Norway points to more factors than just financial, as for instance cultural attributes that encouraged migration and a new openness in society. It is strange that the missionaries did not use the Norwegian-American immigrant experience a few generations earlier as a toolbox when meeting a new and very different culture, although the authors themselves point out that Americans in the 1940s and 1950s would "wince" hearing a relative say something in less than fluent English. The most surprising piece of information was that the Christian mission in Japan was initiated by a military superior, a general. It is interesting to learn to what degree military arguments and military presence were linked to a religious world view in the 1950s. The situation may be the same today.

The book is valuable because of the brief introduction to the theme, the thorough work with sources, and the introduction to cross-cultural theory and the use of it. The analysis of mission activity and questions about traditional missionary assumptions make the book interesting for people in general, as well as for researchers in mission studies and cultural studies.[1]

***Kari G. Hempel** is a historian and Associate Professor of Social Studies at the University of Stavanger, Norway, Department of Early Childhood Education. In her PhD thesis about Norwegian-American churches in the period 1870–1920, she analyzed their transition from being Norwegian to becoming American organizations with Norwegian roots.*

NOTES

1. The author would like to thank cand. philol. Veslemoy Steensnæs Omenaas for help with translation from Norwegian to English.

NOTES FROM THE FIELD

War in the Twentieth Century

SELECTED ARCHIVAL COLLECTIONS

General

Vesterheim, The National Norwegian-American Museum & Heritage Center, Decorah, Iowa: Norwegians in Armed Conflict Collection

The materials in this collection include photographs and papers relating to Norwegian-American participation in the Civil War, World War I, and World War II. The materials relating to World War II include newspaper articles, a pamphlet on Norway during World War II, a photo of a Norwegian cargo ship, and reports on the Camp Little Norway Club of Chicago from 1941 to 1946.

Luther College, Decorah, Iowa: War Letters and Memorabilia, 1861–1972

This collection contains four sub-series: the Civil War, World War I, World War II, and the Vietnam War. Each includes materials such as correspondence, photographs, regalia, published materials, and memorial service programs relating to the war.

World War I

Luther College, Decorah, Iowa: C. K. (Christian Keyser) Preus Presidential Papers, 1866–1951

Christian Keyser Preus was the second president of Luther College. The collection includes letters to and from family, Luther College students, and college and church colleagues. Many of the letters include information about World War I and the Student Army Training Corps (SATC).

Figure 1. Victor Rossing poses with his mother, Helene, following the end of World War I. Rossing wears a uniform with a pin, potentially identified as a marksman's pin. From the Lars A. Rossing Papers, 1866–1963 (P586). Courtesy of the Norwegian-American Historical Association, Northfield, Minnesota.

The Papers of Alfred O. Halvorson, 1904–2013

Alfred O. Halvorson was a 1910 Luther College Preparatory graduate and World War I veteran. Halvorson was born to Norwegian immigrants Helge (Henry) Halvorson and Torbjorg Jonsdatter Tistel Halvorson in Ridgeway, Iowa in 1886. Halvorson enlisted in the Marine Corps in 1917 and was honorably discharged in 1919. The materials in this collection include correspondence from Halvorson during his service, photos, and his military records and honors.

The Papers of David Theodore Nelson, 1922–1969

David Theodore Nelson graduated from Luther College in 1912. He served on Herbert Hoover's Commission for Relief in Belgium in 1914–15 and in the American Ambulance Services in France in 1915–16. The collection includes personal papers, correspondence, biographical papers, and ration cards from World War II.

Minnesota Historical Society, St. Paul, Minnesota: Henry Dahl Military Discharge Certificates, 1892–1913

This collection contains the military discharge certificates of Henry Dahl, who was born in Trondheim, Norway, in 1865 and emigrated to the United States in 1884. He enlisted in the Army in 1887 at Fort Snelling, Minnesota, and left as a quartermaster sergeant in 1918. Dahl died in Minneapolis in 1926. The papers in the collection detail Dahl's thirty-one-year Army career.

Knute Nelson Papers, 1861–1924 (bulk 1916–1923)

Norwegian immigrant Knute Nelson served in the Fourth Wisconsin Cavalry as a soldier in the Civil War, and went on to work in many political positions, including governor of Minnesota (1893–1895) and United States senator (1895–1923). The correspondence and other miscellaneous documents found in the collection highlight Nelson's service during the Civil War and his later political career, including the topic of World War I.

Vesterheim, The National Norwegian-American Museum & Heritage Center, Decorah, Iowa: Edward Beers Collection

Photographs, correspondence, and news articles from Edward Beers's World War I military service are included here.

Washington State Historical Society, Tacoma, Washington: Christian Miller Manuscript

Christian Miller served in the Coast Artillery Corps in the Canal Zone after being drafted in 1918. He was born in Norway in 1896 and emigrated to the United States in 1907 with his parents. The manuscript is entitled "Forward, March?" and consists of all the letters Miller wrote home while serving in the Coast Artillery Corps. It also contains photographs.

Wisconsin Historical Society, Madison, Wisconsin: Magnus Swenson Papers, 1881–1936

Magnus Swenson was a Norwegian immigrant born near Larvik, Norway, in 1854. He emigrated to the United States alone at the age of fourteen, and earned his degree from the University of Wisconsin. During World War I, Swenson chaired the Wisconsin State Council of Defense, and worked as the food administrator for both Wisconsin and northern Europe following the war. The collection includes correspondence, reports, and notices from his time in these positions.

World War II

Luther College, Decorah, Iowa: The Papers of Chellis Evanson, 1914–1993

Chellis Evanson was a Luther College student and history professor who served in the last year of World War I. Series I of the collection contains the World War II Letter Project, completed in 1992. It also includes a rubbing of the project's memorial plaque from 1993. Series II contains issues of *Scuttlebutt,* a newsletter created by Evanson to facilitate communication between Luther servicemen who were separated during the war. Series III contains 707 letters and 1,064 service records from Luther servicemen. Series IV contains the Luther College War Memorial Plaque Campaign files. Series V contains programs and pamphlets relating to the celebration of World War II veterans, including memorial services and wartime commencement programs. Finally, Series IX contains newspapers and other miscellaneous items and memorabilia from World War II.

The Papers of the Rugland Family, 1870–1950

Included here are family letters related to World War II as well as photos, newspaper clippings, and other war memorabilia. The donor, 1959 Luther College graduate Walter Strom Rugland, was a descendant of a Luther College founder.

The Papers of William H. Moe Jr., 1944

This collection contains military papers, correspondence, photographs, and newspaper articles from William H. Moe Jr., including a captured Japanese battle flag from World War II.

Minnesota Historical Society, St. Paul, Minnesota: Harold Knutson Phonodiscs

Several recordings of speeches given by Harold Knutson, a Republican representative in Minnesota from 1917 to 1949, are included in this collection. Knutson was born in Telemark, Norway, and came to the United States with his family at age six. Knutson's speeches address several important topics of the day, including a 1941 speech titled "Neutrality Repeal Means War," in which he opposes the actions of the U.S. military overseas. A few other speeches include Knutson's praise of Norwegian-American efforts in the United States.

Karl F. Rolvaag Papers, 1921–1991 (bulk 1946–1969)

Karl F. Rolvaag, son of author Ole E. Rolvaag, was a Minnesota politician who served as governor of the state (1963–1967) and as the U.S. ambassador to Iceland (1967–1969), among many other positions. The focus of this collection is papers regarding Rolvaag's political life, especially his congressional and gubernatorial campaigns. The collection also contains some materials that detail Rolvaag's time in the Fourth Armored Division.

Norwegian-American Historical Association, Northfield, Minnesota: American Relief for Norway, Inc., Papers

Founded to "relieve distress" among the people of Norway, American Relief for Norway, Inc., was incorporated ten days after the invasion of Norway during World War II and was officially dissolved on December 31, 1946. Correspondence, reports, and publicity material in this collection fall into five categories: clothing drive files, executive secretary's files, president's files, treasurer's files, and corporate records. Topics treated include clothing drives; the collection of funds; the purchase and distribution of food, clothing, shoes, and drugs; publicity; problems with storage and transportation; relations with governments; merging of relief agencies; affiliation with the National War Fund; women's activities; tools for Finmark; and the Anfin O. Sather trust fund for the National Association of Norwegian Agricultural Clubs.

Colonel Bernt Balchen papers, 1899–1973

The materials found in this collection include biographical papers, articles, correspondence, and photographs of aviation pioneer and artist Colonel Bernt Balchen (1899–1973). Balchen was born in Tveit, Norway, and trained in the Norwegian Army before volunteering for Finland's White Army. A top athlete, Balchen was a member of Norway's Olympic boxing team and set records in both cross-country skiing and bicycling. He graduated from the Royal Norwegian Naval Air Force in 1921, and assisted in Amundsen's attempted flight across the North Pole in the dirigible *Norge*. Balchen also served during World War II and played a key role in establishing Little Norway, a training camp located in Ontario, Canada, for Norwegian aviators. In addition, Balchen also taught rescue and survival skills, and ran various operations and ferrying missions during the war.

Figure 2. Prince Harald of Norway sits in a R.N.A.F. Link Trainer at Camp Little Norway in Ontario, Canada, during World War II. Published in *Little Norway in Pictures*, S. J. Reginald Saunders Publisher, Toronto, 1943. From the Camp Little Norway Association Papers, 1941–1947 (P466). Courtesy of the Norwegian-American Historical Association, Northfield, Minnesota.

Esther Gulbrandson Papers

Esther Gulbrandson, a Norwegian instructor at St. Olaf College, was a longtime advocate for Norwegian studies. Gulbrandson's papers in the NAHA collection include information on Camp Little Norway, diaries, family histories, photographs, and correspondence.

Hermana Rye Haugan Papers, 1890–1979

This collection consists of the papers of Hermana Rye Haugan, the widow of journalist and editor Reidar Rye Haugan. Mrs. Haugan was active in many of Chicago's Norwegian organizations and was a leader in relief work for Norway during and after World War II. She was a secretary of the Chicago Working Center for Norway, a sewing and knitting group, from 1944 to 1945.

Jacob Stefferud Papers, 1916–1964

Norwegian immigrant Jacob Stefferud was the chief clerk in the New York and Minneapolis offices of the Norwegian America Line. Stefferud was also acting consul for Norway and a commissioner for Nordmanns-Forbundet. This collection contains miscellaneous papers from Stefferud including correspondence, scrapbooks, and brochures. Also included is a large assortment of records relating to Camp Little Norway, including correspondence, reports, film, photos, and minutes from meetings of the Camp Little Norway Association.

Vesterheim, The National Norwegian-American Museum & Heritage Center, Decorah, Iowa: A. Quisling Collection

This collection contains issues of the World War II magazine *Bilder* from 1945 to 1946.

Raymond Werner Collection

Two certificates of recognition of World War II service from the King of Norway are found in this collection.

Snodgrass Collection

This collection contains 1945 Receipts of Miscellaneous Collections for Pvt. Robert C. Snodgrass from the Finance Department of the War Department, a copy of the ship newspaper *Bienville Bilgewater Bugle* from October 29, 1945, and copies of the *Spearhead* newsletter from the 474th Infantry Regiment.

Vern Asleson Collection

A number of materials relating to the 99th Infantry Battalion, a Norwegian-American battalion during World War II, are found here. These materials include military maps of Germany, newspaper articles, correspondence, lists of veterans, and various stories and information on the battalion.

Vietnam War

Luther College, Decorah, Iowa: The Papers of Harland Nelson, 1960–1994

Harland Nelson, an English professor at Luther College from 1962 to 1992, graduated from Concordia College and received his MA from Washington State University and his PhD from the University of Minnesota. This collection contains academic papers, lectures, course materials, and personal papers from Nelson, including letters to politicians, fundraising documents, and other miscellaneous papers involving the Vietnam War, its effects on the United States and Southeast Asia, and efforts to end the war.

The Papers of Joe Everson, 1969

Letters and other materials relating to the Vietnam War Moratorium comprise the bulk of this collection.